A BUDDHIST APPROACH TO PEACE

A BUDDHIST
APPROACH
TO PEACE

NIKKYO NIWANO

Tokyo • KOSEI PUBLISHING CO.

Translation by Masuo Nezu. The publisher would like to thank Yuri Sōma and Rebecca M. Davis for their editorial assistance. The text of this book is set in monotype Bembo, with handset Perpetua for display. Book design, typography, and layout of illustrations by Rebecca M. Davis.

Passages from the Threefold Lotus Sutra quoted in this book are from *The Threefold Lotus Sutra,* translated by Bunnō Katō, Yoshirō Tamura, and Kōjirō Miyasaka, published in 1975 by John Weatherhill, Inc., New York and Tokyo, and Kōsei Publishing Co., Tokyo.

First English Edition, 1977
Fourth printing, 1982

Published by Kōsei Publishing Co., Kōsei Building, 7-1 Wada 2-chome, Suginami-ku, Tokyo 166. Copyright © 1972, 1977 by Kōsei Publishing Co.; all rights reserved. Printed in Japan.

LCC 79-314995   ISBN 4-333-00308-3

CONTENTS

Preface   7

1. Buddhism: The Teaching of Peace   13

The Lotus Sutra: The Way to Peace, *13* • The Buddha: An
Exemplar of Peace, *14* • Peace in Practice, *18* • On Bearing
Grudges, *24* • Never Compromise the Truth, *26* • Bodhisatt-
vas: Exemplars of the Way, *30*

2. The Peace Teaching of the Lotus Sutra   35

The World View of the Lotus Sutra, *35* • Possibility of Human Development, *38* • Thoughts on Equality in the Lotus
Sutra, *40* • The Nature of Development as Seen in the Parable
of the Prodigal Son, *53* • The Nature of Equality as Seen in
the Parable of the Herbs, *56* • The Parable of the Magic City
That Shows the Way to Peace, *59* • Constructing a Truly
Peaceful Land, *61* • The Whole Lotus Sutra Embodies an Ideology of Peace, *63*

3. Peace Through Religious Cooperation   67

The Essential Meaning of Religion Is Universal, *67* • The

Meaning of Interfaith Cooperation, *70* • Religious Cooperation and World Peace, *73* • Reorienting Our Minds for Peace, *76* • Peace Delegation of Religious Leaders for Banning Nuclear Weapons, *79*

4. Religion and World Peace   85

Impressions of the Vatican, *85* • Encounter with the Unitarians, *88* • Moving Toward the World Conference on Religion and Peace, *90* • The Joy of Sowing Seed, *93* • The First World Conference on Religion and Peace, *106*

5. On the Road to Peace   III

A Tower of Regret and a Tower of Friendship, *111* • The Death of Ideology, *113* • In the Depth of My Heart, *114* • Organizing for Peace, *117* • Transcending Nationalism, *121* • Seventy Years of Gratitude, *123* • Beyond Differences, *125* • Springing from Delusion, *127*

6. A Promising Future   131

Approaching the Second World Conference on Religion and Peace, *131* • Encouraging the United Nations, *133* • Parting the Bamboo Curtain, *135* • Overcoming Difficulties in Realizing the Second World Conference on Religion and Peace, *139* • The Ability to Cooperate with Each Other, *141* • The Practice of Donation, *143* • The Asian Conference on Religion and Peace, *144* • The Boat People Project, *149* • Paving the Way for the Third World Conference on Religion and Peace, *156*

Chronology of Major Activities   157

Monochrome Illustrations, Part One   41

Monochrome Illustrations, Part Two   97

PREFACE

THE DIRECTION OF MY LIFE was decided by the fact that I encountered the Lotus Sutra in the days of my youth. During the first half of my life, I devoted myself wholeheartedly to the dissemination of the Lotus Sutra. In the second half of my life, my activities deepened in the social sphere, widening to an international scope, as I became convinced that the Lotus Sutra is the vehicle of world peace. There is no difference at all in essence, and it is quite a natural process for me as a practicer of the Lotus Sutra, that I devoted myself to disseminating faith during the first half of my life and have focused my energy on the peace movement during the second half.

At a time when we are in the process of preparing for the third World Conference on Religion and Peace after having carried out the first two successfully and meaningfully, I intend to publish this book in the hope of making more widely known the peace ideology of the Lotus Sutra and to reaffirm my determination to strive even harder for peace.

It is said that there are about one hundred institutes for peace in some twenty countries, and that organizations promoting peace activities on an international scale number almost fifteen hundred. I myself am neither an expert on politics, diplomacy, or military matters, nor a professional student of international affairs. However, having been encouraged by the words "There is no expert on peace" of a certain scholar, I intend, from the viewpoint of a man of religion, to think peace, desire peace, and appeal for peace.

Since I began to wrestle with the movement for peace, I have been asked by many fellow believers in my organization various questions, such as "What really is peace? And what should we as people of religion do for the cause of peace?" Through the World Conferences on Religion and Peace, this kind of interest and enthusiasm became deeper and stronger. I tried to answer those questions and appealed for peace through my speeches at various gatherings. I also wrote articles for periodicals, and finally wrote a book, entitled *Heiwa e no Michi,* in Japanese. This is the English edition of that book, containing the major portion of the Japanese version, as well as some original material written especially for this edition.

This book consists of two major parts. The first contains my ideas on peace based upon the Buddhist scriptures, especially the Lotus Sutra. The second part details how I became involved in the peace movement called the World Conference on Religion and Peace, along with my colleagues and with the support of fellow members in my organization, Rissho Kosei-kai. Interreligious cooperation is what I have been advocating since the founding of my organization. I am very happy that I have been able to make the acquaintance of like-minded religious leaders in many parts of the world and also to share in the efforts for peace of people of religion. I hope this modest book will be of some help in the pursuit of world peace.

Nikkyō Niwano
President, Risshō Kōsei-kai
An Organization of Buddhist Laymen

A BUDDHIST APPROACH TO PEACE

I BUDDHISM: THE TEACHING OF PEACE

THE LOTUS SUTRA: Peace is a task for all mankind, but for THE WAY TO PEACE a man of religion it is an even heavier responsibility. Buddhism can be characterized as a religion of peace, and I consider myself, humbly, as a man of peace.

Let me describe some of the influences that have gone into my life to make me a "man of peace." First, I am blessed in having been able to grow up in a country village, surrounded by nature. Second, I was raised in a happy and warm family atmosphere. The third great influence on my life was my encounter with the Lotus Sutra, and it is this experience that I want to share with you.

As I see it, the first and second influences are the elements that have contributed to forming my peaceful nature. But the support and source of strength for that nature has come from my encounter with the Lotus Sutra.

I can still recall my strong excitement when I first encountered the Lotus Sutra. As I listened to the lectures of my revered teacher Sukenobu Arai, I gradually came to understand that this was the very teaching that could make the world one: a pure and peaceful land. Here is the law that saves all people, without exception.

There is absolutely nothing excluded from this teaching —mind, body, individual, society, mountain, river, tree, grass, bird, fish, animal, or insect—everything will be saved. The breadth and boundlessness of the Lotus Sutra is overwhelming!

With that encounter, the whole direction of my life and even the way in which I must live it found a firm basis. Ever since I was introduced to the Lotus Sutra I have had the strength and self-confidence to tackle problems.

Needless to say, in my youth and immaturity, I made my full share of mistakes and experienced the trials we are all heir to. But the one thing that has made me supremely happy is the fact that I was able to gain a self-confidence that won't crack under any difficulty. With the strength and self-confidence that I receive from the Lotus Sutra, I am now, with all my heart and soul, wrestling with the problem of peace.

THE BUDDHA: AN EXEMPLAR OF PEACE   Buddhism in general and the Lotus Sutra in particular are profound teachings on peace. This is because Sakyamuni, the historical Buddha, who expounded the teachings, actually lived his life in accord with the teachings he handed down to us. Sakyamuni Buddha is a true exemplar of peace.

Chapter 12 of the Lotus Sutra tells the story of Devadatta, one of the Buddha's disciples. In one place it says: "The attainment of Perfect Enlightenment, and the widespread saving of the living—all this is due to the good friendship of Devadatta." I was really amazed by these words. Here the Buddha himself says that it is because of his friend

Devadatta that he attained buddhahood and is thereby able to save the whole of mankind. The Buddha further said: "In the future, Devadatta will surely become a buddha."

Besides being a disciple, Devadatta was also a cousin of Sakyamuni Buddha. Even though Devadatta was gifted with a brilliant mind, his heart was warped, and gradually he came to defy the Buddha and finally broke away from the Buddha's community of disciples. Devadatta was not satisfied with merely divorcing himself from the Buddha but took various steps to try to eliminate the Buddha and to decrease his influence.

In an effort to supplant the Buddha, Devadatta attempted to sever the close bonds between the Buddha and King Bimbisara, who deeply revered the Buddha. To achieve his ultimate goal, Devadatta gained the confidence of Prince Ajatasatru, and together they conspired to kill the prince's father. Ajatasatru, agreeing to the scheme, imprisoned the king and let him starve to death. The prince also imprisoned his mother, Queen Vaidehi, who he knew was secretly bringing food to the king. That is how the prince ascended the throne and how Devadatta founded a new religious community with the support of the new king. Devadatta attained his desire.

Because Devadatta had been a disciple of Sakyamuni Buddha for thirty years, he was quite knowledgeable with regard to the Buddha's teaching and he excelled at preaching. By displaying various supernatural powers, he was able to influence the common people and many joined his community, which eventually rivaled the Buddha's in terms of numbers.

Compounding the crimes of murder, slandering the Dharma (the Law), and causing dissension among the Buddha's disciples, Devadatta tried to kill Sakyamuni Buddha. At the time that he conspired with Prince Ajatasatru to kill the prince's father, Devadatta also vowed to destroy the

Buddha. Adhering to his words, he sent thirty-one skilled archers to attack the Buddha; but when they approached the Buddha, they were so awed by his presence that they repented, prostrating themselves before him, and became his disciples.

Next, Devadatta determined to destroy the Buddha by his own hand. One day, intending to strike the Buddha, Devadatta threw a boulder from one of the cliffs of Vulture Peak. On the way down the slope the rock split in two and the smaller piece hit the Buddha's foot. Wounded and suffering great loss of blood, the Buddha bore his pain without complaint and returned to the monastery. After calming those in the monastery who wanted to punish Devadatta, the Buddha lay down quietly. His wound appeared difficult to treat, but it is said that Jivaka, an accomplished physician, cured it surgically.

Devadatta, then certain that it would be impossible to destroy the Buddha through mere human powers, caused an enormous foul-tempered elephant to become drunk, and then stampeded the elephant toward the Buddha as he was begging for alms. The elephant charged the Buddha with an ear-shattering trumpeting. Ananda, one of the Buddha's closest disciples, instinctively attempted to block the elephant's advance. But the Buddha, radiating benevolence, calmly approached the elephant. And it is said that the elephant quite suddenly became gentle and, after kneeling solemnly to the Buddha, turned away.

As time went on, King Ajatasatru grew remorseful over his sins and finally went to the Buddha. There he repented and became a follower of the Buddha's teachings. Having lost his chief patron, the king, Devadatta fell into a miserable existence. One after another his followers deserted him, and no one would give him alms. According to stories of the Buddha's life, Devadatta did many other evil things and eventually reached the point of total despair. After that

Devadatta, though still alive, finally fell into a hell befitting his crimes.

When comparing the evil deeds of Devadatta with the attitude of the Buddha who endured them, we can learn many valuable lessons. In this one story we can observe a range of overt expressions of both violence and nonviolence. Even more plainly, here we can see which is more powerful—violence or nonviolence. And we can see which succeeds.

Also in chapter 12 of the Lotus Sutra, Sakyamuni Buddha relates the story of his life in a previous incarnation.

In this former life, Sakyamuni Buddha was a king; but he was dissatisfied with the ease of his life and constantly longed for the teaching of perfect truth. He declared that he would give anything, including his own life, to possess the knowledge of perfect truth. Finally, he issued a decree stating that whoever could inform the king of such a teaching, a teaching that would save all mankind, would be served all his life by the king.

Soon after that a hermit came to the king and said, "I have a teaching called 'The Lotus Flower of the Wonderful Law' that will save all people. If you are willing to honor all that you promised in your proclamation, I will preach it to you." The king immediately began to serve the hermit. Not only did the king take care of the hermit's meals and all his daily needs, himself drawing the water for the hermit's use, but also he did everything possible to honor and respect his teacher. By making these efforts, he was enabled to hear the supreme teaching.

After relating this story, Sakyamuni Buddha said, "It was thanks to these events in my previous life that I obtained the Buddha's enlightenment. Truly, the hermit at that juncture in my life was no other than Devadatta in a previous life." Then, reiterating his earlier statement, the Buddha said, "The attainment of Perfect Enlightenment, and the widespread saving of the living—all this is due to the friendship of Devadatta." How expansive is the Buddha's mind! This selfless attitude far exceeds anything we might be tempted to call generosity and is far more pure. From this story of only one of the Buddha's previous existences, and from his reaction and acceptance, we can see that selflessness is the most direct path to nirvana—absolute peace.

For the person with a selfless mind like that of Sakyamuni Buddha, everything—good and bad alike—can be a source of enlightenment. It is because of this realization that the selfless person spontaneously expresses his thankfulness for everything in the universe and for all that surrounds him, all that leads him to enlightenment.

We should especially remember that although he was the object of Devadatta's torment, the Buddha never bore a grudge toward Devadatta, nor did he feel the need to fight with Devadatta. From this we can see the true path to absolute peace.

PEACE IN PRACTICE   Among scriptures, a representative example of Sakyamuni Buddha's teaching of the principle of "absolute peace" is the Sutra of King Longevity. The following story is told in this sutra.

Long ago in India, in a country called Kosala, there was a benevolent king known as King Longevity. The people of his country lived in harmony and worked diligently because they heeded the guidance of their king; as a result, their lives were rich and the country was truly peaceful.

However, the king of a neighboring country, Kāsi, was very selfish and envied the prosperity of Kosala. Planning to overwhelm and occupy this prosperous country, he prepared to attack Kosala. Learning of this plan, the ministers of Kosala mobilized their soldiers and made ready to defend their country.

But King Longevity said to his ministers, "I will give

everything in this country—land, buildings, the right to govern, and so forth—to the king of Kāsi." Greatly astonished, the ministers cried out, "O, our king, why do you say this? We will gladly fight and sacrifice our lives for you." King Longevity calmly replied, "If we fight to defend our country, a great number of my people will surely be wounded and killed. I cannot cause such terrible suffering. I cannot bear it." The ministers, still unable to agree, said, "It is odious even to think that this country could be subject to Kāsi."

King Longevity admonished them: "That is limited thinking. Isn't it better to submit to Kāsi than to have tens of thousands of people killed or injured? If we won, many people in Kāsi would be killed. No one anywhere wants to die. No matter what the reason, it is wrong to kill human beings." The retainers said, "We cannot obey this even though it is the order of our king," and left for the border to join their troops.

King Longevity then called the crown prince, his only son, and said, "This will bring death to many people in both countries. I think if both of us disappear the war itself will die. What do you think?" The crown prince replied, "I think so, too, my father." Said his father, "Well, then, let us leave here and hide ourselves in the mountains."

Soon afterward, the news spread throughout the country that the king and the crown prince had disappeared from the castle. The shocked people cried, "They disappeared in order to save us from the misery and suffering of war. What a kindhearted king!" Moved by the compassion of King Longevity, who tried to save numberless lives by sacrificing himself, the ministers unanimously agreed to halt the war, saying, "We are very sorry to have disobeyed the king. But it is not too late. Let us withdraw from the war." They sent their troops home from the front.

Thus a widespread war was avoided and Kosala became part of Kāsi. No one in either country was killed in battle.

However, the king of Kāsi thought that he could not rest until King Longevity was dead. He sent a proclamation throughout the country, saying he would give a generous reward to the person who brought him the head of King Longevity.

At that time King Longevity was living deep in the mountains and leading a hermitlike life. One day, tired from gathering fruit, he stopped beside a path to rest. Before long a ragged old man came by. Because he seldom saw strangers, the king spoke to the traveler. The traveler told him, "I come from a distant country because I long to live in Kosala." The king asked the reason and the traveler answered, "I have always been poor. But I have heard that the king of Kosala is very compassionate and gives alms to those who are poor, and I want to spend my few remaining years there, in comfort."

King Longevity gazed at the old man for a moment and with tears in his eyes said, "As it happens, I am Longevity, the king of Kosala." He then told the old man everything that had happened to him and said, "I am very sorry that I am unable to do anything to help you. I haven't a single penny now. However, I cannot destroy your dream, since you have come such a great distance. I hear that the new king has declared that he will pay a handsome reward to the person who brings him my head. It would be best if you took my head to him."

The traveler was very much surprised and shouted, "You should not say such words! I cannot do such a thing! I will return home. Please hide yourself here." He started to walk toward his old home. Calmly, the king said, "Wait a moment. I shall soon be discovered and killed. If I must die in any case, I would choose to die at the hands of a pure-minded person like you. Please allow me to do this as my last gift."

"Oh, no! I could never do such a heartless thing as murder you."

"Then perhaps you can do something else. Tie me up with a rope and take me to the king. You can do that, can't you?"

The traveler protested, but could not refuse this request. He bound King Longevity and took him to the new king, who was very pleased. The new king gave a bountiful reward to the old traveler and imprisoned King Longevity, whom he decided to execute by burning at the stake.

The young prince, becoming concerned over the disappearance of his father, left the safety of the mountains and came down to a village. Hearing from the villagers of the cruel fate that had befallen his father at the hands of the new king, he was both surprised and resentful. Disguised as a peddler of firewood, he hurried to the palace in order to help his father escape. By the time the young prince reached the castle, his father was already tied to a huge stake and the people were waiting for the fire to be lighted. The prince started to run to his father.

Quickly noticing his son's action, King Longevity looked up to the sky and, as though to himself, murmured, "It is most important for a man to heed the words of his parents. I am not going to die with resentment. I shall die joyfully. If anyone tries to avenge my death, he will soil the purity of my death with the unclean blood of revenge. If one seeks retribution for vengeance through revenge, it leads only to still more vengeance and the chain can never be broken. But if one party forgives the other, then the desire for vengeance will disappear."

When King Longevity had finished speaking, the new king gave his retainers the order to light the fire that would destroy the former king. The prince, who could not bear to witness the sight, ran away to the mountains. However, his resentment was not lessened and he was unable to forgive the new king. Since his father was already dead, he decided to ignore his father's words and seek revenge on the new king.

The prince, posing as a humble, simple man, became a cook for a minister. One day the king was invited to dinner at the minister's house and he found the meal so delicious that he immediately took the prince for his own cook at the palace. The king grew very fond of this young man and planned to promote him to be his close retainer. The king asked, "Have you ever learned swordsmanship?" The prince answered, "I am confident of my technique." The king said, "Then be always by my side and protect me. There is only one enemy I fear, Prince Longevity, the son of King Longevity." Schooling his features so that they did not betray his feelings, the prince answered, "I will gladly protect you at the risk of my life."

The prince was always on the alert for an opportunity to gain his revenge, and the opportunity eventually came. One day he and the king went hunting, and while chasing a stag the two became separated from the rest of the king's party and soon lost their way. Since the prince had lived in the mountains for a long time, he actually knew the way very well, but he pretended that he was quite lost.

By the time they were deep in the forest, the king was completely exhausted. Getting off his horse, the king handed his sword to the prince and said, "I want to sleep for a while. Let me rest my head on your lap." He fell asleep, using the prince's lap as his pillow.

The prince, thinking that this was the perfect opportunity to take revenge, was about to thrust his sword into the king's breast. At that very instant, however, the prince's mind was filled with the last words of his father: "If one seeks retribution for vengeance through revenge, the chain can never be broken."

The prince lost heart and put his sword away. At that

moment the king awoke and said, "Oh, what a nightmare! I dreamed that the son of King Longevity tried to kill me." The young prince reassured him: "Perhaps it is a trick of the mountain demon. Since I am here to protect you, please rest easy."

The king fell asleep again. The prince again took up his sword. Once more the words of his father rang in his mind: "If you seek retribution for vengeance through revenge . . ." The prince's arms grew leaden. Just then the king awoke. "I had another nightmare. Again Prince Longevity tried to kill me." The prince said, "Please do not worry, my lord. It's just your imagination." The king again fell asleep. This would be the last chance. The prince took up his sword and once more his father's words rang clearly in his mind, drowning out all else. At that moment the prince gave up all thought of revenge. The king awoke and said, "Again I dreamed that Prince Longevity had come to kill me. But this time he threw away his sword. What does this mean?"

The prince kneeled before the king and confessed, "In truth, I am Prince Longevity. Three times today I tried to kill you. But each time the last words of my father filled my mind. I could hear only 'If one seeks retribution for vengeance through revenge, it leads only to still more vengeance and the chain can never be broken.' Those words made my hands heavy. O, my king, please kill me. If you do, my everlasting burden will disappear."

The king, who was listening attentively, seemed to have truly awakened for the first time and said, "Is that so? Ah, how wrong I was! Even if I kill you, the burdens of vengeance and revenge may not vanish. But if I apologize from the bottom of my heart, everything will disappear. Everything came about entirely because of a misunderstanding on my part. Please forgive me." The king put his hands on the ground in front of the prince and apologized sincerely.

"O, my king, please rise. I can now forget all that has

happened." The king said, "Oh, can you? Thank you very, very much. I have never before experienced such a wonderful feeling as this."

As the two clasped hands, dawn broke and the light of the morning sun beamed into the forest.

The king returned Kosala to Prince Longevity and went back to his home, saying, "From this time forward, let us live in harmony, like brothers."

The people of Kosala were overjoyed, knowing that the prince was alive, that he would be their new king, and that they would lead happy lives once again.

The merciful and truly peaceable mind of King Longevity lived long in the heart of Prince Longevity and in the hearts of the people of Kosala.

Though this story may seem an absurd fairy tale if we compare it with today's books about peace, I believe that it is a clear example of Sakyamuni Buddha's feelings about peace.

"It is limited thinking to regard sovereignty more highly than the lives of men"; "it is better to sacrifice oneself in order to save many others"; the truth that "if one seeks retribution for vengeance through revenge, the chain can never be broken"—these are important teachings that we should be practicing right now. It seems to me that the Buddha's thoughts and teaching about vengeance, which represent a clear analysis of the human subconscious, are especially important for us today and should be studied often.

ON BEARING GRUDGES In the Dhammapada, Sakyamuni Buddha teaches: " 'He abused me, he beat me, he defeated me, he robbed me,'—In those who harbor such thoughts hatred will never cease. 'He abused me, he beat me, he defeated me, he robbed me,'—in those who do not harbor such thoughts hatred will cease. For hatred does not cease by hatred at any time: hatred ceases by love, this is an unchanging Law."

Here is an immutable truth! Some people may maintain that it is impossible to put this kind of idea into practice today, but I am convinced that it *is* possible. During the 1951 San Francisco peace treaty conference to settle Japan's fate, Mr. Jayewardene, the representative of Ceylon, prefacing his remarks with quotes from the Dhammapada, stated that the country of Ceylon had no intention of seeking war reparations from Japan. Thunderous applause greeted this statement.

Ceylon is known as a Buddhist country. However, in diplomatic relations with other countries, it is impossible for a national government to conduct itself as a religious individual. Threat (overt and implied), deceit, compromise, and so forth are all part of international diplomatic negotiation. Thus, it is all the more impressive that the teachings of the Buddha were so simply stated as the diplomatic policy of a country. When I heard the tremendous ovation that the representatives of the other countries gave the representative of Ceylon, I couldn't help feeling that there was a chance of salvation for all mankind.

What I particularly want to stress is that although Sakyamuni Buddha was thoroughly steeped in the ideal of nonviolence, he never compromised the truth. When he was attacked and injured by Devadatta, he bore it patiently. However, when Devadatta began to teach an intolerable perversion of the truth that had been revealed to Sakyamuni Buddha, the Buddha strongly denounced it and, through his disciple Sariputra, explicitly declared to Devadatta's followers that those who adhered to Devadatta's teaching were opposing the Precious Three (the Buddha, the Law, and the community of believers). Sariputra hesitated to convey the Buddha's displeasure to Devadatta's followers and said, "World-honored One, once I praised Devadatta, therefore

I feel reluctant to reproach his evil now." The Buddha instantly responded, "It is good to praise someone if he has done something praiseworthy. If there is anything for which to be rebuked, be rebuked. Incorrect things should be corrected."

Sariputra withdrew, awed by the Buddha's tenacious respect for the truth. Sariputra immediately went to convey the Buddha's message to Devadatta's followers. Feebly, Devadatta tried to retaliate by accusing the Buddha of living a life of luxury.

Because Sakyamuni Buddha was a thoughtful, warmhearted, and completely peaceable person, he would do nothing to protect his own welfare if it meant distorting the truth. But although he frankly denounced evil as evil, he never held a grudge against any person. This can be clearly seen in his words "due to the good friendship of Devadatta." Even from just the story of his relations with Devadatta, I believe that Sakyamuni Buddha deserves our respect as the supreme exemplar of peace.

NEVER COMPROMISE   Above, I pointed out that Sakyamuni
THE TRUTH   Buddha never compromised the truth.
A clear example of this is found in the following incident related in chapter 5 of the Sutra of the Great Demise (*Mahāparinirvāṇa-sūtra*).

Once upon a time, there was a *bhikshu,* or monk, named Kakutoku, who was eloquent in discourse and widely preached the teaching. *Bhikshus* who were breaking the precepts harbored resentment against Kakutoku, and they tried to harm him with their swords and staffs. Hearing of this, a king named Utoku fought against these bad *bhikshus* to protect the Dharma. Thus he saved Kakutoku from suffering, but the king was badly wounded and eventually died. However, he was reborn in the Pure Land. When the Dharma, the True Law, is being attacked, one must protect the Law in this way.

Of this story, Kāśyapa, one of the leading disciples of the Buddha, asked the Buddha, "Isn't it breaking a precept if a *bhikshu* walks guarded by a believer armed with a sword or a staff?"

Then the Buddha answered, "It is not breaking a precept. Even lay believers carry swords and staffs in order to protect the Right Law. It is not against the precepts. However, even though they carry swords and staffs, they should not kill others."

Because this is an important teaching for us today, we should understand it clearly. In short, it says: "Ordinary people may bear weapons in order to protect the Truth, but they should not kill others." Sakyamuni Buddha never approved of violence, but he did think it a virtue to protect the Right Law by sacrificing oneself like King Utoku. In other words, this teaching affirms that one may resist attack but may never kill.

The way in which Sakyamuni Buddha himself practiced this teaching is seen in the story of something that happened at the time of the Sakya clan's greatest adversity.

Prasenajit, the king of Kosala at the time, deeply respected the serene, serious personality of the Buddha and was devoted to his teaching. Because of these feelings, the king desired to take as his queen a woman from the Sakya clan, and he sent a messenger to the country of Kapilavastu. However, some of the messenger's words were threatening, as when he said, "If you will not freely give us a suitable woman to be queen, we will take one by force." The proud Sakya clan resented these words, but the clan could not oppose the much stronger king of Kosala. They therefore decided to choose a girl who was the child of a wealthy man and one of his humble maids, and to send her to King Prasenajit as the wealthy man's legitimate daughter. The king was very happy to take this girl as his queen.

Before long, the queen conceived and eventually bore a son. The king loved the prince very much; and when the prince, Virudabha, reached the age of eight, the king sent him to Kapilavastu to study archery. While studying archery, Virudabha learned the secret of his heritage when he heard some malicious person say, "He is only the son of a humble maid."

He said to his attending Brahman, "I will seek revenge for this shame. When I ascend the throne, please tell me each day, 'Remember that you were put to shame by the Sakya clan.'" After King Prasenajit died and Prince Virudabha ascended the throne, three times a day the Brahman faithfully recited, "Remember that you were put to shame by the Sakya clan." Thus he inflamed Virudabha's desire for revenge.

The tremendous power of the stimulus of this kind of repetition has been proved by present-day psychology. Recognizing that powerful stimuli can be generated in this way, we can easily imagine the effects of daily worship. Clearly the daily repetition of some devotional service, such as reading or chanting a scripture, would generate a powerful stimulus for the good of all beings.

When the king's desire for revenge, fed by the Brahman's daily reminders, reached its height, he marched his army toward Kapilavastu. Hearing news of this, Sakyamuni Buddha meditated for a while and then stood up and walked to the road that led to Kapilavastu. There he sat quietly under a dead tree.

When King Virudabha arrived, he immediately saw the Buddha and asked, "O, Lord Buddha, why are you sitting beneath a dead tree when there are so many living trees to offer shade?" The Buddha answered, "Yes, my king, it is cool and comfortable beneath the relatives of this tree. But even this dead tree would be the same as the others." The meaning of the Buddha's words is: "Just as even a dead tree wishes to be among its living relatives, as a member of the Sakya clan I also want my fellows to continue to exist." In this way the Buddha preached compassion.

Upon hearing this, the king murmured, "Oh, yes, the World-honored One is from the Sakya clan. I cannot attack Kapilavastu." He thereupon ordered all his troops to return to Kosala.

However, before long the king was again driven to seek revenge and again ordered his troops to march. Once again he found Sakyamuni Buddha sitting under the dead tree. Again the king returned home. This series of events was repeated yet a third time. But when, moved still a fourth time by his desire for revenge, the king arrived in Kapilavastu, the Buddha was nowhere to be seen. It is recorded that Sakyamuni Buddha believed that everything that happens in this world is the fruit of the accumulation of deeds in the past. Thus, everything changes. Knowing that no one can alter this truth, the Buddha abandoned his private feelings of attachment to his clan.

The saying "Three times, even from the Buddha," meaning that a generous act can be repeated no more than three times, originated in this story. The selfless Sakyamuni Buddha was also a warmhearted man. Therefore three times he tried to prevent the destruction of his countrymen. In other words, he tried to move human feelings through the use of human feelings. Although this was effective three times, on the fourth occasion he turned again to the truth of the perfect relationship of cause and effect.

BODHISATTVAS: One of the unexpected lessons I
EXEMPLARS OF THE WAY learned when I was introduced to
the Lotus Sutra was in chapter 20,
"The Bodhisattva Never Despise," where the following
story is found.

Once there was a young *bhikshu* who came to a town
where, with folded hands, he paid respect to everyone he
met, saying, "I deeply revere you. I dare not slight and con-
temn you. Wherefore? Because you all walk in the bodhi-
sattva-way and are to become buddhas." Many among those
who were thus recognized by the monk became angry. They
abused him, saying, "Where did this ignorant *bhikshu* come
from, who takes it on himself to say, 'I do not slight you,'
and who predicts us as destined to become buddhas? We
need no such false prediction."

Although he spent many years constantly being reviled,
he never became irritated or angry, but instead continued to
say, "You are to become buddhas." Whenever he said this,
the people would beat him with clubs, sticks, and stones. But
even while escaping to a safe distance, he still cried back, "I
dare not slight you. You are all to become buddhas."

This young monk, who neither read the scriptures nor
preached, but only paid respect to others by constantly re-
peating, "I dare not slight you," was given the name Never
Despise by the people. Throughout his life Never Despise
continued paying respect to others, and upon drawing close
to death, he was able firmly to grasp the truth of heaven and
earth, human life, and the awesomeness of boundless life.
He was reborn many times and each time preached this truth.
Finally he reached buddhahood.

After telling this story, Sakyamuni Buddha asked, "Can
it be that the Bodhisattva Never Despise was at that time
somebody else? He was really I myself."

The Buddha, in this story of one of his former existences,
explains an important teaching. What is this teaching? It

is the very essence of Buddhism. To recognize the buddha-nature that every living being shares equally and to make an effort to cultivate that buddha-nature are basic and essential aspects of Buddhism that must be fully understood before one can invite all mankind to share in the Buddha's total teaching and before any kind of universally serene or peaceful existence can be established on this earth. The teaching in this chapter is also an excellent guide to perfecting one's character.

It was not until long after reading "The Bodhisattva Never Despise" that I realized the true meaning of this teaching. When I first read this chapter, I was deeply moved by the wonderful way of life chosen by Never Despise. At first I was impressed by his steadfastly practicing one thing —respectful commendation of everyone he met—without losing patience. Then I was impressed by his courage in following his convictions and by the fact that even though he was abused by others he did not return the abuse. Never Despise's way of life was one that was tender in personal relations but firm in defending the truth. He was a man both brave and peaceable who was a genuine expert on life, as well.

In the Lotus Sutra the teaching of nonviolence is clearly stated by bodhisattvas in the following pledge found in chapter 13, "Exhortation to Hold Firm":

"But we, revering and believing in the Buddha,
Will wear the armor of perseverance;
For the sake of preaching this sutra
We will endure all these hard things.
We will not love body and life,
But only care for the supreme Way.
We will, throughout all ages to come,
Guard what the Buddha bequeaths.
World-honored One! Thou knowest that,

In the corrupt age, vicious *bhikshus,*
Knowing not the laws so tactfully preached
As opportunity served by the Buddha,
Will abuse and frown upon us;
Repeatedly shall we be driven out,
And exiled afar from the monasteries.
Such evils will be our ills
For remembering the Buddha's command,
But [we] will endure all these things.
Wherever in villages and cities
There be those who seek after the Law,
We will all go there and
Preach the Law bequeathed by the Buddha.
We are the World-honored One's apostles
And, amidst a multitude having nothing to fear,
Will rightly preach the Law.
Be pleased, O Buddha, to abide in peace."

To suffer any hardship for the sake of the Law and not only to endure hardship patiently but also to go anywhere and actively preach the Law—this is the very essence of the practice of the apostles of peace who are devoted to non-violence. This spirit is expressed in the words, "We will not love body and life, / But only care for the supreme Way." This is the attitude of one who lives in truth and dies in peace, thinking, "It is most regrettable that there is even a single person who is not touched by this supreme teaching. When compared with this teaching, one's life is not significant."

This spirit has moved man the world over. In Asia, one man who truly exemplified this spirit was Mahatma Gandhi. He was fatally wounded by a Hindu who blamed him for the partition of India. When Gandhi was being carried away on a stretcher, because he couldn't speak he formed with his hand the mudra known in Japanese as *semui* just before he died. The meaning of this mudra is "to give a power that is fearless according to the truth." In the Lotus Sutra this is explained in detail in chapter 25, "The All-Sidedness of the Bodhisattva Regarder of the Cries of the World." The mudra *semui* is formed by raising the open right hand to the chest with the palm facing out, directed to the person being recognized. This mudra is often seen in portrayals of Sakyamuni Buddha.

Perhaps in the *semui* Gandhi was manifesting both his willingness to forgive his assassin and his freedom from fear of the wound. Gandhi should be looked upon as a person who lived his life in the true spirit of the teaching in the Lotus Sutra: "We will not love body and life, / But only care for the supreme Way."

2 THE PEACE TEACHING OF THE LOTUS SUTRA

THE WORLD VIEW
OF THE LOTUS SUTRA
I would like to discuss briefly the world view of the Lotus Sutra. At the beginning of both the Sutra of Innumerable Meanings and the Lotus Sutra, mention is made of the congregation that gathers to listen to the Buddha preach.

These opening paragraphs explain that there were present not only many bodhisattvas but also *bhikshus* (monks) and *bhikshuṇīs* (nuns), *upāsakas* (male lay devotees) and *upāsikās* (female lay devotees), people of high class (kings, princes, and ministers) who were not yet believers, and members of the general public, all of whom were seated on an equal level. In addition, there were gods who live in heaven (the spiritual world), demons who fly in the sky, dragons who abide in the water, and many other beings. In other words, there were gathered all the living creatures in the whole universe, all equal in the great assembly present at the preaching.

This constitutes a symbol of the world view of the Lotus Sutra, which, if I may summarize it briefly, would be as follows:

There is a single, invisible entity that is embodied in all things existing in our universe. This is the great life force of the universe. All things in this world fundamentally are of this one entity. Therefore, though phenomena appear in infinite variety, essentially they are equal in their existence.

"The Reality of All Existence" or the "Ten Suchnesses" is the law that explains this world view theoretically. Thus, chapter 2 notes that "only a buddha together with a buddha can fathom the Reality of All Existence, that is to say, all existence has such a form, such a nature, such an embodiment, such a potency, such a function, such a primary cause, such a secondary cause, such an effect, such a recompense, and such a complete fundamental whole."

What does the Reality of All Existence mean? It has two major meanings. One is that there is a single, invisible entity that is embodied in all things, as mentioned above. The other is that the true form of everything is its actual appearance. In other words, the teaching of the Reality of All Existence tells us first to discern the real state of all things (the entity) that is behind all phenomena and second, to clearly recognize the actual appearance of all things.

To go into further detail concerning the Ten Suchnesses: each phenomenon has its inherent form, inherent nature, inherent embodiment, and inherent power (potential energy). When potential energy begins to function in various ways according to its primary cause (cause) and secondary cause (conditions), an effect (result) and recompense (enduring influence) will be produced that follow exactly from the primary and secondary causes. This is the phenomenal, real state of all things of this world, in other words, the form of all things as they are.

However, at the end of this teaching, the Buddha preaches

"such a complete fundamental whole." This signifies that there is a single, invisible entity that exists in everything, as mentioned earlier. In other words, though various phenomena and their changes appear multifarious, all are facets of a single universal truth. Their fundamental nature is *śūnyatā* (voidness), in which all things are completely equal.

Though the word "voidness" does not appear in the original text, it means that from the beginning to end, everything is always equal in its real entity; it is nothing other than voidness.

Voidness is the only one, real existence that makes everything and every phenomenon of the universe. Scientifically speaking, it is the fundamental energy that is manifested in all phenomena, and religiously speaking, it is the great life force that permeates everything that exists in the universe, namely, the Eternal, Original Buddha.

As this explanation may be difficult to understand in relation to our daily lives, it would perhaps be better to explain it in the following way. First, if the real embodiment of all things is a single entity, it becomes understandable that all mankind, over four billion people, each with a unique appearance, fundamentally forms one single existence. When one can fully realize this, then fraternal love, the feeling that all human beings are brothers and sisters, will spring up in one's heart. One will be filled with a sense of harmony and cooperation. This sentiment of fraternity is the benevolence or compassion taught in Buddhism. Friendship based on this great sense of oneness with others is the very essence of benevolence. The Japanese word *jihi* is the equivalent of benevolence or compassion. The character *ji* is a Chinese translation of the Sanskrit word *maitreya,* an abstract noun derived from *maitri,* which means "utmost friendship." *Hi* is a Chinese translation of the Sanskrit word *karuna,* whose original meaning is said to be "moan." When one sees others moaning in suffering or agony, one cannot refrain from moaning oneself. This state of being sensitive to the pain of others and feeling it as one's own is called *hi*. Both *ji* and *hi* are elements of the pure friendship that springs spontaneously from the sense of oneness, the lack of a barrier between oneself and others.

If all people in the world had this sense of *jihi* (benevolence), how could they hate or have ill feelings toward others? How could they fight wars? A benevolent spirit is the true starting point of peace. Peace without benevolence is a false or transient peace.

The reason I emphasize that the Lotus Sutra teaches peace is that the teaching of the Reality of All Existence, which demonstrates the philosophical basis of the peace ideology of the sutra, is based on a spirit of boundless benevolence. Now, when pondering the statement "everything is the same in its entity," doesn't it follow that each human being, although quite different in outward appearance, is essentially equal in his or her existence? How can it be otherwise?

The egalitarian view of man expounded by the Lotus Sutra is based on the truth of this fundamental existence. It does not force the position that one should ethically think of and see others as equal. Rather, the view springs from a deep realization of the true nature of the universe. As such, it is deep-rooted, firm, and constant through all phenomenal changes. The spirit of the equality of all human beings, which is one of the main pillars upon which world peace must be built, is I believe solidly endorsed by the Lotus Sutra.

POSSIBILITY OF HUMAN DEVELOPMENT The Law of the Reality of All Existence, or the Ten Suchnesses, preaches not only the basic equality of man but also that one's phenomenal situation can be changed in any way according to one's mental attitude. In other words, these laws also teach the equality of potential development.

We human beings all have our own personal qualities (character, talents, disposition, and so on), inherent form, nature, embodiment, potency, and function. However, even these sprang originally from the entity of the universe, so that they never exist in a fixed state. When a certain cause (primary cause or direct cause) and certain conditions or occasion (secondary cause) are given, the appropriate result (effect) and influence (recompense) will appear.

Therefore, in the human mind there exists the potential to fall into hell as well as to rise to the state of buddhahood. Thus, the attainment of buddhahood taught in the Lotus Sutra means to perfect one's personality and to reach the stage of the highest awakening. It does not signify that to become a buddha means becoming a deity far beyond humanity. This is a most important point. In other words, the attainment of buddhahood means to perfect one's real form as man, the form of man as it is.

We must seriously consider the meaning of the phrase "as it is." We human beings, though originally sacred and beautiful in our existence, which is at one with the great life force of the universe, now exist in a tainted condition far from this fundamental existence. But if we comprehend the truth taught by the Buddha and improve our minds and deeds in accordance with the truth, someday we will be able to manifest this original form in our bodies. This is what is called the attainment of buddhahood.

What a wonderful thing it is that every human being is given such a possibility. We tend to think, "I can't change myself." But we should realize that this is not so; we *can* change ourselves if we try hard enough. We even can become buddhas. Knowing this vast capacity for change, we can feel strong hope and courage.

If we realize the idea of the Reality of All Existence, or

the Ten Suchnesses, our eyes, that is, our way of seeing others, will also begin to change. Most important, we will be able to see the equal buddha-nature (potential to become a buddha) within the personalities of others. And we come to respect those whom we have despised or considered quite incapable: "This person too has infinite potential." Human respect cannot be said to be real unless it reaches this stage.

T'ien-t'ai Chih-i, the third patriarch in the lineage of the Chinese T'ien-t'ai school of Buddhism, who lived in the sixth century, taught "Three Thousand Realms in One Mind," interpreting liberally the possibility of change and the flow of humanity taught in the Law of the Ten Suchnesses. That is, the "three thousand realms" will change in accordance with one's spiritual attitude. "Three thousand" simply means "numerous," and the statement as a whole means that by our attitudes we can change our environment in any way. I believe that true world peace is based upon this truth.

THOUGHTS ON EQUALITY
IN THE LOTUS SUTRA
Now let us consider some of the thoughts on true equality that are found in the Lotus Sutra. This sutra teaches us of unlimited possibilities: in it we learn that not only man but every living and nonliving thing can attain buddhahood. This is stated in chapter 5, "The Parable of the Herbs," where the Buddha says to his disciple Kāśyapa:

"Kāśyapa; you have well proclaimed the real merits of the *Tathāgata*. Truly they are as you have said. The *Tathāgata*, in addition, has infinite, boundless, innumerable merits, which if you spoke of for infinite *koṭis* of *kalpas* you could not fully express. Know, Kāśyapa! The *Tathāgata* is the king of the Law. Whatever he declares is wholly free from falsity. He expounds all the laws by wise tactfulness. The Law preached by him all leads to the stage of perfect

The peace activities of men of religion begin with prayer.

The first WCRP was convened at the Kyoto International Conference Hall in October, 1970.

Mr. Sean MacBride (Ireland), Nobel Peace Prize laureate, chaired the Human Rights Commission.

Left, Dr. Eugene C. Blake, then General Secretary of the WCC, greets the author.

Three hundred participants and two thousand visitors from thirty-nine countries listened to addresses.

Dr. Ralph D. Abernathy (U.S.) affectionately greets Rev. Niwano.

Archbishop Helder Camara (Brazil) said in his speech that "it is a miracle accomplished by the Lord that we are here."

In December, 1970, after WCRP I, the author visited South Vietnam and helped distribute relief goods to the suffering people.

He also appealed to the people to promote religious cooperation in order to make a unified effort for peace.

Rev. Niwano visited Mr. Kurt Waldheim, Secretary-General of the U.N., at his office in November of 1973, and handed him a copy of the proceedings of WCRP I.

The author talks with Mr. Gustav Heinemann (right), President of West Germany, in Bonn in August of 1972.

In April, 1974, Rev. Niwano was invited to China and, at the Guang Ji Si Temple in Peking, talked with religious leaders.

◄ At Peking Air Port the author is seen off by Mr. Chao Pu-chu (at author's right), president of the Buddhist Association of China.

The author visited Romania and Hungary, where Executive Committee Meetings of IARF were held in May, 1974.

Children always symbolize a bright future.

knowledge. The *Tathāgata* sees and knows what is the good of all the laws and also knows what all living beings in their inmost hearts are doing; he penetrates them without hindrance. Moreover, in regard to all laws, having the utmost understanding of them, he reveals to all living beings the wisdom of perfect knowledge.

"Kāśyapa! Suppose, in the three-thousand-great-thousandfold world there are growing on the mountains, along the rivers and streams, in the valleys and on the land, plants, trees, thickets, forests, and medicinal herbs of various and numerous kinds, with names and colors all different. A dense cloud, spreading over and everywhere covering the whole three-thousand-great-thousandfold world, pours down its rain equally at the same time. Its moisture universally fertilizes the plants, trees, thickets, forests, and medicinal herbs, with their tiny roots, tiny stalks, tiny twigs, tiny leaves, their medium-sized roots, medium stalks, medium twigs, medium leaves, their big roots, big stalks, big twigs, and big leaves; every tree big or little, according to its superior, middle, or lower capacity, receives its share. From the rain of the one cloud each according to the nature of its kind acquires its development, opening its blossoms and bearing its fruit. Though produced in one soil and moistened by the same rain, yet these plants and trees are all different.

"Know, Kāśyapa! The *Tathāgata* is also like this; he appears in the world like the rising of that great cloud. Universally he extends his great call over the world of gods, men, and *asuras,* just as that great cloud everywhere covers the three-thousand-great-thousandfold region. . . .

"Just as that great cloud, raining on all the plants, trees, thickets, forests, and medicinal herbs, and according to the nature of their seed perfectly fertilizing them so that each grows and develops, so the Law preached by the *Tathāgata* is of one form and flavor, that is to say, deliverance, abandonment, extinction, and finally the attainment of perfect knowledge. If there be living beings who hear the Law of the *Tathāgata* and keep, read, recite, and practice it as preached by him, their achievements will not enable them to understand their own nature. Wherefore? Because there is only the *Tathāgata* who knows the seed, the form, the embodiment, and the nature of all these living beings, what things they are reflecting over, what things they are thinking, what things practicing, how reflecting, how thinking, how practicing, by what laws reflecting, by what laws thinking, by what laws practicing, and by what laws attaining to what laws. There is only the *Tathāgata* who in reality sees, clearly and without hindrance, the stages in which all living beings are, just as those plants, trees, thickets, forests, medicinal herbs, and others do not know their own natures, superior, middle, or inferior. The *Tathāgata* knows this unitary essential Law, that is to say, deliverance, abandonment, extinction, final nirvana of eternal tranquillity, ending in return to the void. The Buddha, knowing this and observing the dispositions of all living beings, supports and protects them."

It is clear that ability and temperament differ from one individual to another. This is seen in our differing backgrounds, states of health, environments, occupations, and so forth. Since such conditional differences exist, the way of receiving or perceiving the "rain of truth" differs from one person to another, even though everyone possesses the identical buddha-nature. However, regardless of the ways in which receiving the truth may differ, all people are quite equal because one receives the rain of truth in accordance with one's innate capacity and grows in accordance with one's innate nature, opening distinctive blossoms and bearing distinctive fruit.

Please consider this last sentence carefully. It expresses the concept that to manifest completely the innate nature unique to that individual being is, in fact, the attainment of buddhahood for that being. On the surface this seems to teach the equality of the potential for human attainment of buddhahood; however, on a deeper level we find the boundless teaching of the attainment of buddhahood by all things in the universe. "All things" includes birds, beasts, insects, and fish, trees and grasses, and even such nonliving beings as soil, stones, water, and air—in short, all forms of existence.

On hearing that even nonhuman existences can attain buddhahood, you might at first think it strange; but when you recall the truth of the Reality of All Existence, it is not at all peculiar. All things in the universe are part of a fundamental whole; that is to say, all things are created from "voidness," which is of one flavor, so that everything originally comes from but one source. Therefore, it cannot be that only man can attain buddhahood while other living and nonliving things cannot. Moreover, when we fully realize that to attain buddhahood means to manifest completely one's unique innate nature, whatever this may be, the idea of the attainment of buddhahood by all things of the universe is not at all strange.

This idea can also be stated as follows: "Even plants and earth can become buddhas because all beings, sentient and nonsentient, have the buddha-nature." Here we find a thoroughgoing compassion based on a comprehensive view of equality not seen in any other religion. This is the teaching that holds that man should not long only for the attainment of his own buddhahood but also for that of all things in the universe and that he should, in all his actions, express this compassion toward all things in the universe.

Since everything that exists is the manifestation or embodiment of the great life of the universe (the Eternal, Original Buddha), if we consider with clear minds we can understand that both a violent mountain storm and a gentle valley stream are products of the great life of the universe. Because all forms, both sentient and nonsentient, are manifestations of this reality, any form that can manifest the complete embodiment of its distinctive innate nature has in fact achieved buddhahood. A tree that has manifested completely the buddha-nature unique to that tree has just as surely attained buddhahood as any human being who has perfected the buddha-nature unique to him.

In today's world we tend to forget this truth. We selfishly harm, contaminate, and destroy nature, stealing from it its innate form. It is as though we arrogantly feel that our existence is superior to that of animals, plants, and the earth. This is in fact the taking of the "life" of nature and is also the heinous act of preventing those animals and plants and even the earth from attaining the buddhahood that they have the potential to achieve.

What is the result of such killing? If we prevent others from attaining buddhahood, that is to say, if we thwart the perfect manifestation of the innate nature of others, our actions will finally rebound upon us alone. According to the principle that nothing has an independent ego, it cannot be otherwise. An obvious proof of this principle is to be seen in the so-called civilized nations, where people are now suffering the effects of environmental pollution.

Man is an element of nature, an integral part of nature. Therefore, if man destroys nature, he will surely destroy himself. It is high time that we human beings freed ourselves from our narrow, shortsighted, selfish idea that it is sufficient that mankind alone be happy. It is time for us to return to the spirit of the Lotus Sutra, which teaches us to live in harmony with nature and with other beings, letting each form of existence fulfill its potential to perfect its own buddha-nature.

THE NATURE OF DEVELOPMENT AS SEEN IN THE PARABLE OF THE PRODIGAL SON   Reverend Toyohiko Kagawa, who is regarded as one of the most active Christians in modern Japan, praises the Lotus Sutra in very high terms in his book *Religion as Life,* which contains the phrase "the mind affecting the tiniest one [the smallest and weakest existence]." This phrase appears to reflect the strong impression that the parable of the prodigal son in "Faith Discernment," chapter 4 of the Lotus Sutra, has made on Kagawa. This chapter is indeed profound and moving because it expounds the true bodhisattva spirit of respecting and loving even the smallest existence and of helping each existence, however small, to develop its own buddha-nature.

Briefly, this is the parable. There was once a man who, in his youth, left his father and ran away from home. For fifty years he wandered from place to place, growing poorer with each passing year, while each year his father grew more and more prosperous. Wandering through village after village and passing through countless cities and countries, the son at last reached a city where there was a magnificent mansion. On approaching this mansion, he saw a noble man, who looked almost like a king, being waited on by many attendants and servants. The poor man, seeing this rich man possessed of such great power, became very frightened and quickly ran away. The rich man was, in fact, the poor man's father.

The father, who had never ceased thinking of his son, immediately recognized as his son the poor man standing outside the gate of the mansion and instantly sent his attendants to rush after the man and bring him back. The poor son, surprised and frightened, thought that even though he was innocent of any wrongdoing, he was about to be imprisoned, which would certainly mean his death. Thinking this, he became all the more terrified and fainted, falling to the ground. Seeing this from afar, the father knew at once that his son's disposition was weak and that his own lordly position had distressed his son. Some days later, the father sent two lowly, mournful-looking men to offer his son a job carrying earth, directing the men to say: "There is a place for you to work here; you will be given double wages." The son accepted the job and the father was overjoyed by the return of his son.

Sometime later, the rich man put on coarse, ragged, dirty clothes in order not to arouse fear in his son's mind again. In this way he was able to approach his son and speak kindly to him. After making generous provisions for his son's welfare, he said, "From this time forth you shall be as my own begotten son." The poor son, though rejoicing at this treatment, still thought of himself as a lowly hired laborer. For this reason, the son patiently continued his humble work of carrying earth for twenty years. During this period, mutual confidence grew between the rich man and his son and the son went in and out of his father's house with freedom, even though he still lived in his original simple quarters. The rich man gradually gave his son more and more responsibility and finally made his son manager of his entire estate. All this time, the son's ideas and horizons gradually grew larger and his will became well developed. The father, knowing of these changes, called his son to a meeting attended by the king and the leaders of the city and there announced: "This is really my son and I am really his father. Now all the wealth that I possess belongs entirely to my son." For the first time, the prodigal son knew that the rich man was his natural father and, at the same time, that the boundless wealth of his father was his own. The son's joy was immeasurable.

The teaching contained in this parable is that the relationship between the Buddha who is the great life of the universe (that is, the Eternal, Original Buddha) and us human beings is, in fact, that of a single existence, even though we generally try to create a separation, as when we use such phrases as "the Buddha and living beings." The prodigal son (living beings) considered the rich man, who was in truth his father, to be some separate existence because he didn't realize that even though he wandered away from the house of his father (the Buddha) he could return to it again. However, when he was able to comprehend that the rich man and his father were one and the same person, his rejoicing was quite natural.

The teachings from the beginning of the Sutra of Innumerable Meanings through the second chapter of the Lotus Sutra are presented rather philosophically and scientifically, as is seen in the explanation that it is "voidness" that creates all things and all phenomena. But in the parable of the burning house in chapter 3, "A Parable," and in the parable of the prodigal son in chapter 4, "Faith Discernment," the fundamental existence that is the basis of all existence is presented allegorically, personified as a living, breathing existence called "father." And in chapter 16, "Revelation of the [Eternal] Life of the Tathāgata," this fundamental existence is identified as the Eternal, Original Buddha, who not only embodies the great fundamental nature of the universe, but as supreme teacher exemplifies the Buddhist outlook on the world.

On the surface, "voidness" may seem to be a cold, unclear entity. But if we think of it as "the father of every living thing" or "the eternal life that permeates the universe," we instantly sense the relationship that it has to us warmblooded beings. We sense the vigorous, changing rhythm of both heaven and earth. When we finally understand that we are part of this eternal force, that we are its natural, living children, we can experience no stronger joy. There is no deeper peace of mind. There is no greater confidence.

The parable of the prodigal son teaches us these things.

What causes us to feel deep gratitude is not only the realization that the essence of this teaching is so precious, but also the realization that through his deep affection and wisdom the rich man helps the son to awaken to his worth and dignity and to develop his talents at his own speed. We should seriously contemplate this affection and wisdom, and try to learn from them. In the Nirvana Sutra we read: "Worldly laws do not contradict the teachings of the Buddha." The teachings of the Buddha (the Buddha-laws) are also worldly or secular laws. In today's world there are many countries whose histories resemble the story of the prodigal son. If we, with great affection and wisdom, can help those countries awaken to their own worth and dignity and can encourage them to develop their own abilities and natures to the full, then we will see peace come to the world at last.

The developed countries, which have just this mission, are also like the prodigal son. At best they have reached only the stage comparable to that reached by the son when he became manager of his father's estate. It seems to me that the truly important task facing all countries, both developing and developed, is to awaken to their individual inherent natures and for each to develop its talents according to its own potential.

THE NATURE OF EQUALITY AS SEEN IN THE PARABLE OF THE HERBS   As mentioned earlier, the Lotus Sutra is filled with the teaching of fundamental equality. The story of the attainment of buddhahood by the daughter of a dragon king in chapter 12, "Devadatta," and the belief expressed in chapter 5, "The Parable of the Herbs," that plants and earth can also become buddhas because all beings, both sentient and nonsentient, have the buddha-nature are but two examples.

If we apply this teaching to our own global society, it is

apparent that all peoples have equal buddha-nature, equal potential to attain buddhahood. Even though some cultures may appear to lag far behind others, to be greatly undeveloped, even primitive, there is no basic difference between the people of one culture and another. All mankind has the potential to attain buddhahood. Therefore, if a person will but follow the truth with conviction, he can surely manifest his own fundamental nature clearly and can fully develop his innate talents.

We should be careful here not to misinterpret "equal in potential" as being the same as "equal in manifestation." This kind of misinterpretation is called "the concept of erroneous equality," and we cannot calculate the damage such thinking has done to the hopes of peace for our society. When we consider the process of the true fundamental nature of the phenomenal world, we can easily understand that such thinking has no basis in fact.

Although all things of this world derive their existence from the same source, "voidness," or, more scientifically, "energy," their appearances are greatly varied: there are both living things and nonliving things. Living things range from simple amoebae to the most complex plants and animals, including man. When these numerous living and nonliving things fully develop their innate natures and talents, and completely fulfill their inherent roles, total harmony will be achieved. This kind of harmony is called nirvana, or absolute peace.

The idea that being equal in potential means the same thing as being equal in manifestation is obviously in conflict with the scheme of nature. If we could change our society, forcing it to accord with this erroneous idea, the world would be filled with people having the same face, the same physical form, the same nature, and the same talents, and we would find our society very monotonous indeed. But fortunately this is not the case. The true essence of equality is to have a high regard for the equality of human rights and potential, and to develop and utilize fully the inherent talents unique to each of us while maintaining respect for the differences among all beings.

This important concept is made very clear in chapter 5, "The Parable of the Herbs," which states that "from the rain of the one cloud [each living plant] according to the nature of its kind acquires its development." We should consider this carefully.

Aren't we currently experiencing great difficulties because of a misunderstanding of the true nature of human society and even of the true nature of a nation? For example, because of the limited thinking which maintains that the only proper form of "development" is the industrialization of developing countries, there is a worldwide tendency to attempt to mold developing countries into replicas of already developed countries. But is this a valid goal? Needless to say, the most urgent task at hand is to take whatever measures are necessary in order to relieve the suffering in developing nations. Let the countries now at war lay down their arms. Let the soldiers of the countries involved withdraw from the battle front. Let the developed nations come to the aid of the developing nations that are suffering severe shortages of food and medicines. It is absolutely essential that we restore at least a temporary peace by taking these steps. However, the real work begins after this. Each country should be encouraged to achieve its maximum growth according to its unique potential. And when each country has sufficiently developed its own fundamental nature, we will find that all nations can coexist without infringing upon each other's rights, that international relations are smooth, and that harmony has been achieved. We would then have found, for the first time, the lasting peace we have sought so long.

THE PARABLE OF THE Chapter 7 of the Lotus Sutra,
MAGIC CITY THAT SHOWS "The Parable of the Magic City,"
THE WAY TO PEACE clearly teaches that a temporary
peace is a negative kind of peace,
and that lasting peace is the peace of positive creation and
harmony. The parable goes as follows:

In a certain country there was a very long hard road,
menaced by ferocious beasts and many other dangers. There
was a multitude who wished to pass along this perilous way,
seeking a most valuable treasure that was said to be found at
the end of the road. Among the multitude was a strong
leader, wise, clearheaded, and resolute, who in peril saved
all from danger. But the people all became exhausted and
told the leader, "We are weary and worn out and want to
turn back." The leader knew *hoben,* the way of guiding
people properly in accordance with circumstances, and re-
flected thus: "These people should be pitied. How can they
want to turn back and miss such a great treasure?" He
thought of a device: "Let me use my supernatural power
and make a great magic city, splendidly adorned with hous-
es, surrounded with gardens and groves, streamlets and bath-
ing pools, massive gates and lofty towers, full of both men
and women." Having performed this transformation, he
pacified the people, saying, "Do not fear! Enter, all of you,
into this city and let each enjoy himself at will." When the
people had entered the city, their hearts were full of joy.
All thought only of rest and ease and believed they had been
saved. When the leader knew they were rested, he called
them together and addressed them, saying, "Let all of us
push forward! This was only an illusory city. I saw that
you were all worn out and wanting to turn back midway.
I, therefore, by a device, temporarily made this city. Now
we must diligently advance together to the Place of Jewels."
So saying, the leader encouraged the people and led them

to the end of the road so that they could gain the jewels.

This parable directly teaches the practice of Buddhism, but at the same time teaches the road of life and the way that shows the path to world peace. The long and hard way symbolizes the long history of mankind's suffering caused by war, starvation, poverty, the violation of human rights, and so on. In order to get rid of such suffering, it is necessary to enter the peaceful city as a temporary measure. Unless it recovers from exhaustion and reinvigorates itself, mankind may fall into madness. Such a "peaceful city" is the symbol of a warless state, a state of generally pleasant life, that is, a "temporary peace." However, this warless state alone is not real peace. It is not possible to live safely forever in such a temporary peace, even if one wishes to, because this state is not a firmly rooted peace but only a temporary respite. Like the visionary castle, it is destined to disappear someday.

Real, lasting peace is far beyond this. It is important that every human being and the various organizations formed by people abandon their wayward greed and move positively forward to the work of creation suitable for each according to the will of the universe. This means to do work appropriate to the individual, and thereby to create ceaselessly those things that make oneself, others, and society as a whole happy. Such works of creation will surely produce a kind of large-scale harmony. Like an orchestra, such constant creation produces spontaneous harmony—this is lasting peace, the most precious jewel of mankind.

Though temporary peace is absolutely indispensable, it is merely a step in the process. Man should move beyond this to the way to lasting peace, using a temporary peace as a resting place. To do this, reformation of one's mind by religion is indispensable.

CONSTRUCTING A TRULY PEACEFUL LAND   The spirit of the Lotus Sutra does not aim solely at the salvation of individuals or at the awakening of individuals to the truth, but ultimately aims at changing all of society to the right Law. This is symbolized by the words "to purify the buddha-land," which appear frequently in the Lotus Sutra.

Chapter 11, "Beholding the Precious Stupa," in particular, strongly emphasizes this. In this chapter, we are told of how various buddhas take the dirt of the *sahā*-world (this world of suffering) three times and change it to a Pure Land. This first occurs when the buddhas from all directions go to the *sahā*-world and pay homage to Sakyamuni Buddha and to the Precious Stupa of the *Tathāgata* Abundant Treasures. The sutra says, "Thereupon the *sahā*-world instantly became pure."

It takes place a second time when Sakyamuni Buddha is about to convene his emanated buddhas from all directions. "Then Sakyamuni Buddha, desiring to make room for the buddhas who had emanated from himself, in each of the eight directions of space, transformed two hundred myriad *koṭis* of *nayutas* of domains, making all of them pure."

The third time this happens is when the buddhas from the ten directions are about to assemble. "Sakyamuni Buddha, in order that the buddhas who were coming might be seated, in each of the eight directions, transformed two hundred myriad *koṭis* of *nayutas* of domains, making them all pure."

The reason the land is repeatedly purified is that there is no world other than this world where buddhas abide, and that, even so, the truth cannot be implemented while the world is as stained as it actually is. Therefore, in order to welcome the truth and bring it into the world, the land must first be purified.

In the world of faith, people often feel, "Since this world

was originally the buddha-land, if one reaches enlightenment in his mind, the world will naturally become the
Pure Land." Strictly speaking, this view is related to the
selfish belief that "it is enough if I myself am enlightened,
if I alone become happy."

The Lotus Sutra asserts that, in order for man to become
truly happy, in addition to individual enlightenment and
happiness in one's individual life, it is necessary to purify the
nation (society), thus going a step further. It is in the spirit
of the Lotus Sutra for a person to make efforts not to escape
from actuality but rather to positively wrestle with it and
strive to purify it.

Chapter 15, "Springing Up out of the Earth," demands this
effort from ordinary people. When the bodhisattvas who
had come from other lands spoke to the Buddha, saying,
"If the Buddha will allow us, we will stay in this *sahā*-world
and preach this sutra abroad in this land," the Buddha answered, "Enough! My good sons! There is no need for you
to protect and keep this sutra. In my *sahā*-world there are
bodhisattvas who are able to protect and keep, read and recite, and preach abroad this sutra." When the Buddha had
thus spoken, all the earth of the three-thousand-great-thousandfold realm of the *sahā*-world trembled and quaked, and
from its midst there issued innumerable thousand-myriad
koṭis of bodhisattvas.

It is a great mistake to think of these bodhisattvas as
saviors or as beings who have come from another world,
since really they are symbols of people who live on this
earth. However, this does not mean "people" unconditionally; it must mean "people who are awakened to the Truth
and who practice the Truth." This is the point of the chapter.

The fact that the *Tathāgata* did not give in to the plea of
bodhisattvas who came from other worlds teaches us that
this very earth should be made peaceful by the efforts of

the people who are living on it, and they should create their happy lives with their own hands.

The fact that the bodhisattvas issued forth from the midst of the earth can serve as a very important lesson. The person who wants to make this world peaceful should directly touch the suffering of the ordinary people in actual society, coming down to the level of the general public, even though his own mind may be highly enlightened. We also learn that one cannot save others by idealism alone; one must grapple with actual problems.

There is another important lesson. The names of the four leaders of the bodhisattvas springing up out of the earth contain the word "conduct": Eminent Conduct, Boundless Conduct, Pure Conduct, and Steadfast Conduct. That is to say, those who put the truth of Buddhism into the practice of benevolence are very real bodhisattvas; without such action (or movement), peace cannot be realized in this world. Needless to say, the "bodhisattvas" are not limited to the Four Great Bodhisattvas: "All the earth of the three-thousand-great-thousandfold realm of the *sahā*-world trembled and quaked, and from its midst there issued together innumerable thousand-myriad *koṭis* of bodhisattvas." These countless bodhisattvas are all bodhisattvas of "practice." They are nothing other than practicers of the Lotus Sutra.

THE WHOLE LOTUS SUTRA
EMBODIES AN IDEOLOGY OF PEACE
The teachings on peace in the Lotus Sutra are countless, since the whole of the Lotus Sutra presents a concept of peace. I would like to summarize by discussing the conclusion of chapter 21, "The Divine Power of the Tathāgata," which is a symbolic recapitulation of the ideas of the Lotus Sutra.

In this chapter, it is explained that the Buddha reveals divine power and shows various mysterious or miraculous phenomena, all of which symbolize the truth that everything is one.

Near the end of the chapter, after revealing various miraculous phenomena, we read: "[Then] with various flowers, incense, garlands, canopies, as well as personal ornaments, gems, and wonderful things, they all from afar strewed the *sahā*-world. The things so strewn from every quarter were like gathering clouds, transforming into a jeweled canopy, covering all the place above the buddhas." This means that all living things in the universe paid homage to Sakyamuni Buddha and the other buddhas.

There are various ways of performing *pujana* (veneration), such as presenting flowers, incense, and votive offerings. However, the highest veneration is to make each act one of meeting the mind of the Buddha. There is nothing that pleases the Buddha more, or for which he is more thankful. That all the treasures were transformed into a jeweled canopy indicates that all the living things of the worlds in all directions uniformly paid homage in this highest manner. And at the same time, this predicts that though at present people's behavior is varied, including both good and evil, in the future it will coincide at the point where all behavior meets the mind of the Buddha.

Thus, when the ground is covered by the beautiful canopy, the last mysterious phenomenon takes place. There is no distinction among the worlds in all directions and anyone can go anywhere quite freely; the whole universe becomes one buddha-land.

This phenomenon, called "one buddha-land," symbolizes the following. At present, there is a clear distinction between worlds: the *sahā*-world is filled with illusions, while in the heavenly Pure Land there is no suffering at all and hell is a world of great agony. However, when the time comes that all people live according to the truth taught by the Buddha, such distinctions as heaven, *sahā*-world, and hell will disappear and all the worlds of the universe will be united as one buddha-land.

This is the "one buddha-land" of spiritual life; and if spiritual life reaches this state, the actual world cannot but change accordingly. That is to say, a world of great harmony will appear when all nations, all races, and all classes come to live in accordance with the one truth, so that discrimination among them vanishes, discord and fighting do not occur, and all the people work joyfully, enjoy their lives, and promote culture. In short, the whole world will become one buddha-land.

Organizationally speaking, it can be said that the buddha-land means the formation of a world federation. Therefore, the symbolic meaning of the revelations appearing in chapter 21, "The Divine Power of the Tathāgata," portrays a realistic idea and must be said to be a most encouraging prophecy for us.

3 PEACE THROUGH RELI-GIOUS COOPERATION

THE ESSENTIAL MEANING OF RELIGION IS UNIVERSAL My humble efforts for peace are based on interfaith cooperation, and this cooperation is based on the idea that the essential meaning of every religion is essentially the same. This idea is taught clearly in the Lotus Sutra.

In chapter 21, "The Divine Power of the Tathāgata," one finds the following passage: "At the same time all the gods in the sky sang with exalted voices: 'Beyond these infinite, boundless hundreds of thousands of myriads of koṭis of asaṃkhyeya worlds, there is a realm named sahā. In its midst is a buddha, whose name is Sakyamuni. Now, for the sake of all bodhisattva-mahāsattvas, he preaches the Great-vehicle Sutra called the Lotus Flower of the Wonderful Law, the Law by which bodhisattvas are instructed and which the buddhas watch over and keep in mind. You should with all your utmost heart joyfully follow it and should pay homage and make offerings to Sakyamuni Buddha.' "

"The Lotus Flower of the Wonderful Law" is the foremost and most wonderful teaching, which, though existing in the secular world, is not tainted with its depravity—just like the lotus flower that blooms in the mud—and shows people how they can lead pure and free lives.

"The Law by which bodhisattvas are instructed" literally means the teaching that is preached in order to instruct bodhisattvas. However, in the present context, it can also be interpreted as the teaching that instructs one how to reach the stage of the highest awakening through the practice of acting with benevolence toward all others, as well as elevating oneself spiritually.

"The Law which the buddhas watch over and keep in mind" means the teaching that buddhas (those who have attained enlightenment) have treasured as the utmost truth and have protected, that it might receive only its right dissemination.

These three phrases explain directly the content, purpose, and value of the Lotus Sutra. However, as we begin to understand from the above explanation, the Lotus Sutra, in its deepest meaning, is not a proper noun but a common noun meaning the highest and most real teaching, which teaches the truth of the universe to all human beings and leads them to the true way of living.

But the real and the highest teaching can never be two. Though it can be expressed in various ways, in its fundamental meaning it is one.

Therefore "the Great-vehicle Sutra called the Lotus Flower of the Wonderful Law, the Law by which bodhisattvas are instructed and which the buddhas watch over and keep in mind" indicates neither that the Lotus Sutra is a proper noun nor that the object of worship and veneration, the *Tathāgata* Sakyamuni, is a proper noun. Accordingly, if we interpret the paragraph in a broader sense, citing the words of all the deities in this universe—"Take refuge in this teaching and pay homage to Sakyamuni Buddha"—this cannot but be the following prediction: "At present, there exist various kinds of teachings in this *sahā*-world, and that fact prevents mankind from finding the way to a common happiness. However, in the future, every teaching and study will surely come to be united in one teaching, in one truth. At that time, this *sahā*-world will become the most holy place in the whole universe."

At present, teachings that ought to uplift people instead face in various directions, and each religion or denomination has selfish or exclusive ideas or sentiments that prevent unity.

Also, in the area of politics, which ought to bring comfort to people's lives, various ideas confront each other with no regard for the general public, who are essential to the body politic. The result is to increase people's suffering instead of bring comfort to their lives, and even to bring them dangerously close to ruin.

The same thing can be said of learning. Learning, which was originally intended to promote the welfare of the people, has degenerated to a learning of subhuman standard; a learning for honor and profit; a learning that does not bring happiness to people because they have excessively divided it into narrow, specialized branches and forgotten its fundamental spirit. The most tragic example of this may be the nuclear bomb, which, although it was originally planned to be the most valuable product of atomic physics, could exterminate all mankind. This is an example of technology cooperating with the devil.

When these various religions, thoughts, and sciences unite in the spirit of respecting truth, respecting human beings, and respecting the harmony that was preached by Sakyamuni Buddha, the ideal pure land will be realized on earth: a high spiritual culture as well as an advanced material civilization will fully bloom and the *sahā*-world will become the center of the universe in the true sense.

This is the idea preached in this chapter: in the future, all teachings will unite in one original, fundamental meaning. Taken from the past, this chapter indicates that in the future all teachings will become one. When I came to know this chapter, "The Divine Power of the Tathāgata," I began to feel deeply the essential oneness of religion and made this realization the creed of my religious activity.

THE MEANING OF INTERFAITH COOPERATION Now I would like to discuss the meaning of religious cooperation and the interfaith activities we have been involved in. After World War II, many new religions were born in Japan and developed vigorously. Though there were valid reasons for their prosperity and vigor, these new religious organizations were attacked and even persecuted. As the proverbs say, "Forwardness will cause trouble" and "A tall tree catches much wind." Some of the weaker organizations were not able to defend themselves. Rissho Kosei-kai also suffered much slander and persecution.

At that time, a suggestion was made that the new religious organizations form a federation, and such a movement was begun. I agreed with it and joined the movement from the beginning. The Union of the New Religious Organizations in Japan (UNROJ) was established in October, 1951.

The number of affiliated organizations was then 24; however, outsiders looked at the union skeptically, saying, "A gathering of founders can never function smoothly, as they all think themselves the sole representatives of the 'true faith.' There will be much quarreling soon." On the contrary, just the opposite turned out to be true. Our meetings were very harmonious and cheerful, so that the "expectations" of the outsiders proved to be quite wrong.

However, as I was too idealistic, I tried to go too fast

and suggested that all the member organizations open up their doctrines and learn from one another. But as Mr. Tokuchika Miki, President of the Perfect Liberty organization, warned me, "If we try to deal with one another's doctrines, a very difficult situation may arise." He was right.

Between ideal and actuality there is a great gap that can be closed only over a period of time. I gradually came to realize this. My own thinking is as follows.

When seeking the origin of this great universe and the various elements and living things that exist therein, we come to see the one and only energy. This energy functions variously and creates all things and all phenomena. Buddhism calls this fundamental energy the "void," while some scientists call it "Planck's constant." Whatever it is called, it must be the life of the universe itself and cannot be thought to be otherwise.

It is not easy for ordinary people to understand why we call this fundamental life force that creates all things the "void," energy, or Planck's constant. It is intangible and difficult to grasp. People cannot sense that they live within a world created and sustained by this energy. Therefore Buddhism calls this fundamental life force "Buddha" and Christianity calls it "God"; Judaism, "Yahweh"; Islam, "Allah."

Accordingly, as far as being right goes, for all great religions (we except low religions that deal with fetish or idol worship) it can be said that the great, original object of all faiths is one.

Why, then, are there so many different religions in the world? It is not necessary to make a complex problem out of this. The answer is that the various races and peoples developed independently, making them small communities unto themselves. From primitive times, each community has had its own *kami* (supreme being or beings). In some cases, these *kami* were the spirits that guarded individuals, the village, and the tribe; in other cases, *kami* meant the fundamental life force of the universe. The former, needless to say, is a *kami* that applies only to a specific group, while the latter must be one which is universal, even when examined to its very roots.

In the days when transportation was undeveloped and communication between different communities was very difficult, people could not understand this essence, and as the name of the supreme being was different and the rituals were also different, people thought that they all believed in different supreme beings. Therefore, many people believed that religions other than their own were heresy or paganism; it was too difficult to understand their oneness and achieve harmony. Not only was it difficult to understand and harmonize with one another, but also many religious wars were fought, and many people have died in ridiculous battles waged in the name of one god or another.

But this is now changing. The world has become smaller and smaller with the development of transportation and mass communication. Gradually, the thinking of people throughout the world is tending toward a common thought. This tendency will continue to grow. It is an anachronism that, even in such an age as this, all religions stand alone and still have exclusive natures.

No religion that thinks of the supreme being as being its own protective deity, or guardian deity, deserves to be considered a religion for present and future societies, though it may be valuable from the viewpoint of folklore. Even such a protective deity, when we examine it and look into its fundamental nature, must be an offshoot of the one life of the universe.

When the world was divided into so many groups and communication among them was so limited, it was necessary that many offshoots exist. But in the future, when the global human community becomes a reality, doctrinal isolationism of the sort that says, "This is our guardian deity;

it has nothing to do with you," will, I believe, gradually vanish in the spiritual world.

Basing my activities on such an idea, for some years I have earnestly proclaimed religious unification. However, I have come to realize that it is an idea which can only be realized a couple of centuries from now, and that the word "unification" easily becomes so misunderstood that I fear many will try to counteract this movement.

Because of the behavior and deeds of "tribal" religions, which have been stained with the corpses of innocents whose spilled blood has merged for hundreds and even thousands of years, it is difficult for people to conceive of any kind of union.

Therefore I have decided to use the term "religious co-operation" or "interfaith cooperation" as a temporary stage toward reaching the goal, and have made every effort for its advocacy and implementation today.

I wish to add here that religious cooperation does not mean only that various religious bodies and individual religionists cooperate for specific purposes in terms of practice. For example, it is not enough that religious bodies cooperate in charity campaigns for the suffering people of the world. It does not mean such superficial cooperation but rather a mutual understanding from the bottom of the heart; a shaking of hands for the cause of the common issues of man—otherwise, religion can never achieve the great task of realizing world peace and promoting the happiness of all mankind.

RELIGIOUS COOPERATION AND WORLD PEACE In essence, every great world religion preaches love for mankind and tries to provide peace of mind. Religious believers generally have a far stronger love for mankind and desire for peace than those lacking faith.

Furthermore, they know how to show this desire for peace and love for man in their actions. Therefore I firmly believe that people of religion possess the greatest ability to join together and transcend differences of race and nationality. With this strong belief, I have been doing my utmost to strengthen religious cooperation. Religious cooperation is nothing other than building a strong fort of peace on the foundation of a deep understanding of our common humanity.

There are some who assert that it is hardest of all for religious people to cooperate with one another. And looking back on the history of the narrow self-righteousness and exclusiveness of people of many faiths, this cannot be altogether denied. However, this apparent contradiction, this historic failure of religions to work together for peace, stems from the fact that until recently, religious people attached importance only to formal differences of faiths, without trying to see the common aspects that lie behind their respective religions. I believe that such narrowness would disappear if they endeavored to think about the *essential* meaning of all religions. This would help open their minds.

When we observe or think about living things and various concepts, there are two methods that we can apply: we can note the differences or we look for the common aspects.

Take human beings, for example. We can define a given person as an Anglo-Saxon man or a Mongolian woman, according to differences of physiognomy, physique, skin color, language, or customs. This emphasizes the differences. On the other hand, if we emphasized common points, we would quickly see that every man and woman has two eyes, one mouth, two legs, and two hands. Affection of parents toward children, and fear of starvation and death do not vary from race to race.

For scientific researchers, the former way of seeing things is unavoidable. However, people in general tend to use it excessively. And, in comparing differences, unfavorable observations are bound to be made. The worst result of this type of thinking is to become discriminatory toward anything different. For instance, one may decide, "He thinks differently from me. Therefore I don't want to have anything to do with him." Unwillingness to associate may be acceptable, but if this becomes an antagonistic sentiment, it can be very dangerous.

Let us take a completely different example. Are the facial features, dispositions, ways of thinking, hobbies, occupations, and lives of your friends exactly the same as yours? Probably not. But still you remain friendly with them. You can smile at criticism if it is from a friend, but not if it is made by others. You would not eat a slice of bread already partly eaten by a stranger, but if it were partly eaten by a close friend you would probably be willing to finish it.

Why? Because you have a sense of oneness with your friend. Various differences, such as disposition, race, and religion, are not on your mind. This sense of oneness—"We are good friends," or "We are on good terms"—occupies the largest part of your awareness. I think that we need to define better how human beings should live—concrete goals for mankind—based on the realities and needs of our everyday lives.

In order for people to live peacefully and on good terms with one another, we must learn to emphasize the common aspects of mankind rather than our differences. This is not, however, a new thought—it was taught by Sakyamuni Buddha over twenty-five hundred years ago.

This concept can be clearly seen in the Sutra of Innumerable Meanings: "All laws were originally, will be, and are in themselves void in nature and form; they are neither great nor small, neither appearing nor disappearing, neither fixed nor movable, and neither advancing nor retreating; and they are nondualistic, just emptiness. All living beings, however, discriminate falsely: 'It is this' or 'it is that,' and 'it is advantageous' or 'it is disadvantageous'; they entertain evil thoughts, make various evil karmas, and [thus] transmigrate within the six realms of existence; and they suffer all manner of miseries, and cannot escape from there during infinite *koṭis* of *kalpas*."

If we look seriously at the state of the human world today, we can only agree. Through the division of wealth, classes confront each other; out of the greed of materialism, nations fight each other; in the traditional sentiment of discrimination, races battle each other; and because of differences of ideas and organizations, groups of nations antagonize each other. Troubles are never-ending. If we leave things as they are, we can have no guarantee of peace against the looming threat of nuclear war. Humanity is now facing a terrible crisis.

What can save mankind from this crisis, from this miserable situation? In order to find peace, we all must reorient our way of thinking in order to work together. There is no other way to establish lasting peace on earth, to change this hellish stage completely, than to reorient our minds, to restore our souls. Sakyamuni Buddha expounded, "The three worlds of desire, form, and formlessness are the products of the mind."

REORIENTING OUR MINDS FOR PEACE   Even when it becomes clear that the reshaping of our world perspective is necessary for attaining lasting peace, how can we accomplish this difficult task? It seems to me that there is no way other than through the understanding that man is originally the "same"; everything is, in essence, one. This is based on the principle that I discussed earlier in detail. The Sutra of Innumerable Meanings, as quoted above, preaches it philosophically. The Lotus Sutra, which traditionally accompanies the Sutra of Innumerable Meanings, expounds much more intelligibly the idea that "every man is the child of the Buddha." The Buddha in this sense means the great life of the universe, which is the very root of all phenomena. In other words, the Lotus Sutra teaches that even though the individual person appears to live a detached existence, fundamentally everybody is an offshoot of the one great life of the universe—we are all brothers and sisters.

This important concept is taught only by religion. No science teaches it. And insofar as religion is the sole teacher of this truth, it is absolutely indispensable for peace. There are many sciences, such as sociology, anthropology, ecology, and physiology, which teach how people *do* live, but there is nothing aside from religion to teach how man *should* live. Therefore I have been advocating faith for all men and religious cooperation as my lifelong task.

Every religion contains the teaching that "man is originally one." Christianity teaches that everything was created by Almighty God. For Christians the concept of Almighty God, creator of the universe, is often misconstrued as an image of human form with human emotions, though He has divine powers. Such a God cannot be reconciled with human reasoning. But is it not possible that the God who created the cosmos, the God most people believe in, and the Universal Life Force of Buddhism are all different manifestations of the same Reality?

Shinto prayer refers to "The Sovereign Ancestral *Kami* who divinely remain in the high Heavenly Plain." Superficially one might interpret this to mean that many gods and goddesses gather in a specific place called the high Heavenly Plain. But the meaning in its essence and truth is that this universe is full of gods, or *kami*. "Full of *kami*" means that I am a *kami*, you are a *kami*, trees and flowers are *kami*—everything is an offshoot of *kami*.

In chapter 11 of the Lotus Sutra, "Beholding the Precious Stupa," it is explained that each direction was filled with buddha-*tathāgatas* from its four hundred myriad *koṭis* of *nayutas* of domains. In chapter 16, "Revelation of the [Eternal] Life of the Tathāgata," the Buddha teaches: "Throughout *asaṃkhyeya kalpas* / [I am] always on the Divine Vulture Peak / And in every other dwelling place. / When all the living see, at the *kalpa*'s end, / The conflagration when it is burning, / Tranquil is this realm of mine, / Ever filled with heavenly beings."

In the Shingon sect of Buddhism, it is taught that the three-thousand-great-thousandfold world is the body of the *Tathāgata Mahāvairocana*. The mandala expresses that the forms of various buddhas and bodhisattvas, the offshoots of the *tathāgata,* are omnipresent in the universe.

The roots of the name of the Amita Buddha of the Pure Land Sect and of the True Pure Land Sect include the words *Amitābha* (Infinite Light) and *Amitāyus* (Infinite Life). This means that the Amita Buddha does not abide solely in the "western Pure Land" (paradise) but that the Amita Buddha is in fact eternal, imperishable life that exists everywhere and is the light that illuminates all the corners of this universe.

Please reflect deeply on the meaning behind such truths as God Almighty, creator of the universe; the Sovereign Ancestral *Kami* who divinely remain in the high Heavenly Plain; the root of the universe is the Eternal, Original Buddha; the three-thousand-great-thousandfold world is the body of the *Tathāgata Mahāvairocana;* and *Amitābha, Amitāyus.* It may be understood that all these truths are rooted in the same Truth.

Although ways of expression and nuances in the way of thinking differ according to the land, time, and race into which a religion was born, the fundamental teaching is, in its essence, the same. If we were to dispute over details, we could find minor differences between the *agape* of Christianity, the compassion of Buddhism, and the *makoto* of Shinto. But when we examine their roots, all are human sentiments that are, simply and purely, the great life of the universe.

If the believers of every religion were to study very deeply the true meanings of their respective religions, they might all discover behind the various differences of expression the truths that man is one and that to live on good terms with others is the way of living that coincides with the truth.

When all people on earth can fathom the fundamental truth of human existence and can restore their souls and reorient their minds away from discrimination and toward a sense of oneness, true peace and real happiness will come to this world for the first time.

The religious cooperation that I advocate does not stop at the shaking of hands by people of different religions but aims at reaching the stage where by studying in depth the true meaning of various religions, one can fathom the truth common to each religion and, by grasping this common truth, perceive oneness spontaneously.

PEACE DELEGATION OF RELIGIOUS LEADERS FOR BANNING NUCLEAR WEAPONS The trend toward interreligious cooperation is becoming stronger and stronger. In its early period, the UNROJ (Union of the New Religious Organizations in Japan) was criticized as a movement of people without principles, who had forgotten the uniqueness of religion, and that therefore would soon disintegrate. That was over twenty years ago. Sympathizers increased year after year, and the number of affiliated organizations reached eighty-six as of 1972—and all the members are active and on good terms.

The UNROJ became affiliated with the Japan Religions League a year after its own formation. Since then, the post of chairman of the Board of Directors of the Japan Religions League has rotated among the representatives of the five affiliated unions: the Japan Buddhist Federation, the Japan Christian Federation, the Association of Shinto Shrines, the Association of Sectarian Shinto, and the Union of the New Religious Organizations in Japan. I took the chairmanship of the Board of Directors of the UNROJ in October, 1965, and I am now serving my sixth term. I was also the chairman of the Board of Directors of the Japan Religions League in 1969 and 1974.

The affiliation of the UNROJ with the Japan Religions League was a landmark in the days when the ecumenical movement was young and established religions viewed new religions with antagonism. Today this antagonism no longer exists, and both traditional and new religions are cooperating. The ultimate inevitability of the unity of all religions is, however slowly, on its way to realization.

Internationally, the ecumenical movement has also been gaining strength. My first opportunity to meet foreign religious leaders for the promotion of interfaith dialogue came in 1963 when I visited some Western countries as a member of the Peace Delegation of Religious Leaders for Banning Nuclear Weapons. I was especially attracted by this delegation's mission of calling on religious people from both East and West to stand up for peace together, hand in hand.

The sixteen-member delegation, headed by Masatoshi Matsushita, then president of Saint Paul University in Tokyo, and the Reverend Rosen Takashina as honorary head (I was one of the vice-heads), first flew to Rome for a special meeting with the Pope and handed him the following Peace Proposal.

PEACE PROPOSAL

Thanks to the firmness and sincerity of the governments of the United States, the United Kingdom, and the USSR, and the supreme support of the nations concerned, the Partial Test-Ban Treaty will be the saving grace of the whole of mankind.

Even though the nuclear nations still share a mutual distrust and retain fundamental differences in world view and world policy, the fact that the Partial Test-Ban Treaty was concluded is a sign that the human race has taken its first step forward from darkness to light, from ruin to coexistence. Here we can rediscover human wisdom and renew our shining hope for the future of mankind. We religious people recognize a great invisible power behind this historical decision, and are thankful for it.

On this joyful occasion, we propose the following three points with the aim of continuing the movement of the world toward peace:

1) To ban totally and unconditionally the testing of nuclear weapons.

2) To ban totally the production, preservation, and use of nuclear weapons.

3) Through the peaceful utilization of atomic power based on international cooperation, to overcome the unequal distribution of wealth and to promote the welfare of all the peoples of the world.

We strongly feel that the total cooperation of religious people around the world is necessary in order to realize the above proposals. We appeal to religious leaders everywhere to join in a worldwide effort to ban atomic weapons forever.

September, 1963
Peace Delegation of Religious
Leaders for Banning Nuclear
Weapons

The Pope said in reply: "I would like to express my deep respect and gratitude to you all, who have come from afar with the great aim of banning nuclear weapons and realizing world peace. Especially when I think that among you are important leaders who represent Japanese religious circles, it is my great joy that you have visited me. I totally agree with your peace declaration.

"Nuclear arms are terrible weapons that threaten the survival of mankind. As people of religion, we have a responsibility to try to abolish nuclear weapons totally and to save mankind from the danger of war. Your three-point Peace Proposal properly expresses the desires of mankind, and I promise you that I will seriously meditate on these points.

"I do not have direct power to affect either politics or economics. What I can do is to call upon the minds of people. I will endeavor to do so in order that the three points of your Peace Proposal may be realized. I sincerely hope that as men of religion, you will continue your efforts for peace."

From the Vatican the delegation flew to Geneva, Switzerland, and talked with Secretary-General Visser't Hooft of the World Council of Churches. I was greatly impressed by the Secretary-General's words: "Many people seem to think that real peace is far above us and that small efforts are useless. But that kind of thinking is not only pessimistic about what we can do on earth, it is also wrong."

After that, the delegation visited France, the USSR, West Germany, Britain, and the United States. However, as the main purpose of the delegation was the total banning of nuclear weapons, the government leaders of those countries seemed wary of meeting us. We could not meet with top leaders, such as Premier Kruschev of the USSR or President Kennedy of the United States, but we were able to talk with many key figures, including Secretary-General U Thant of the United Nations, Patriarch Emillian Elinov of the Orthodox Church in the USSR, Dr. Michael Ramsey, Archbishop of Canterbury, Mr. Alexander of the Department of Defense of the U.S.A., the Foreign Secretary of Britain, and Etienne Manac'h, the head of the Asia Bureau of the Foreign Ministry of France.

Everyone expressed his agreement with our proposals, though each differed in the way he expressed it. But, as if in unison, all said to us that our country, the only "atomically baptized" nation, should take the initiative in the movement to ban nuclear weapons. I strongly felt that, in order to change to happiness the misery of suffering caused from the atomic bombs, in order to console the souls of A-bomb victims, and in order never to repeat this horrible tragedy, the role that we Japanese are to play is extremely important.

The Peace Delegation did another important thing. As a byproduct of this mission, many religious people understood and cooperated with each other in purpose and action, transcending sectarianism far more than they had ever anticipated. I sensed at that time that the day of the religious cooperation that I had been advocating was dawning, and I felt inexpressible joy. I recollect these words without being able to remember who said them: "One can do nothing alone—but until one makes a start, nothing at all can be done."

4 RELIGION AND WORLD PEACE

IMPRESSIONS OF THE VATICAN   Paul Cardinal Marella came to Japan from the Vatican in March, 1965 as a special envoy of the Pope to meet with the leaders of various Japanese religions and visit various religious organizations. While here he invited me to the Second Vatican Council as a special guest representing Japanese religious circles. The Vatican Council is the highest assembly of the Catholic Church, at which the Pope and the bishops of the church decide the guidelines and direction of the church. The participants are limited to the bishops of the Catholic Church under the leadership of the Pope. At the First Vatican Council, in 1869–70, the doctrine of papal infallibility was decided.

Recently, however, great changes have been taking place in Christianity. As is well known, since the Reformation sparked by Martin Luther in 1517, Christianity has been roughly divided into Catholics and Protestants. Hatred between the two sides sometimes even caused wars. There is nothing more irrational than conflict among religions—

which, after all, are meant to purify people's minds and bring peace to the world. Some people who had the mentality to overcome this irrationality began the ecumenical movement, and it has been gradually growing.

Under such circumstances, the late Pope John XXIII declared, "Those who have been saved by the blood of Christ should not fight each other; on the contrary, they should plan to get together and work for peace." Pope John made great contributions to the promotion of the ecumenical movement, and his successor, Pope Paul VI, has continued to move Christianity toward reconciliation. He himself opened up the heavy doors sealing the Vatican and visited Patriarch Athenagoras of the Greek Orthodox Church and other Christian leaders, and even set up a liaison office for non-Christian religions, making a special effort to promote mutual understanding among different religions. And finally, in a bold decision, he invited a Buddhist to the Vatican Council.

In 1965, I attended the opening ceremony of the council on the morning of September 14. Thirty minutes prior to the opening, 2,500 bishops, who were gathered from all over the world, were solemnly seated in order in Saint Peter's Basilica.

At nine o'clock, the 132-meter-high dome was filled with the beautiful sound of a hymn, and Pope Paul VI appeared in his white robes, bathed in rainbow light from the stained-glass windows and surrounded by the cardinals. He celebrated mass solemnly in the center of the main hall.

I was given a seat by the side of the altar, so that I could observe the ceremony very well. I was deeply impressed by its solemnity and magnificence. I felt strongly that religion must be correct in its theology but, at the same time, must be accompanied by beautiful and solemn religious rites in order to deepen the emotion of "faith." In Buddhism we even have a saying, "Faith stems from solemnity."

At the beginning of his speech at the opening of the

council, the Pope said, "We unanimously desire to forge stronger bonds of union with those Christian brethren who are still separated from us. We mean to address to the world a heartfelt message of friendship and salvation. With humble and firm confidence we expect from the divine mercy all the graces which, though undeserved, are necessary for us to fulfill our pastoral mission with loving and generous dedication." He spoke with humility but also with awareness of his position as the Pope, who serves on behalf of Christ. This attitude, I think, is one all people of religion must achieve.

The Pope spoke for about an hour, mainly about peace and ecumenism.

On the evening of the following day, I personally met and talked with the Pope. I will always remember that day, and especially the words the Pope said to me, shaking my hands warmly: "I know what you are doing for interfaith cooperation. It is very wonderful. Please continue to promote such a wonderful movement. . . . In the Vatican, too, the attitude toward non-Christian religions is changing. It is important for people of religion not to cling to factions or denominations but to recognize each other and pray for each other." My heart was greatly warmed by those words. Buddhists pray for Christians and Christians pray for Buddhists—this is the very spirit of religious cooperation. I was very much impressed.

I said to the Pope with the deepest sincerity, "I will work to my utmost for world peace."

At the end of the meeting, the Pope said to me vigorously, "God will surely bless you in your holy work." I felt the truth in his voice, and new courage sprang up in my heart.

I will never forget the warm hands of Pope Paul VI. I believe that our firm handshake put blood into the cooperation, friendship, and mutual understanding between Christianity and Buddhism. It was my utmost joy that we totally agreed on the necessity of religious cooperation. I deepened my determination to be a bridge between the two religions, and extend this bridge to various other religions, as well.

On the way back to the hotel after meeting the Pope, I thought that Buddhism and Christianity must come from the same source. There is no difference between the compassion of Buddhism and the love of Christianity. Basically, they teach us to forgive each other, to be tolerant and openminded, to exercise mutual warmth and caring, and to lead happy and peaceful lives.

The morality taught in Buddhism and Christianity is quite similar too: do not kill, do not lie, do not be greedy, do not commit adultery, be patient, and so on.

Sakyamuni Buddha teaches in the Lotus Sutra that there are not two or three true teachings: there is only one. All teachings are the one Buddha-vehicle, the one Truth. There in the Vatican, I felt an affirmation of the truth and the world. It can be said that at that time I finally became able to cherish hope of the possibility of holding a peace conference at which all religious leaders in the world would gather to discuss world peace.

ENCOUNTER WITH THE UNITARIANS When I visited various countries as a member of the Peace Delegation of Religious Leaders for Banning Nuclear Weapons, Rissho Kosei-kai came into contact with the Unitarians of America. When I understood the viewpoint of the Unitarians I felt strongly encouraged by the fact that there were people in the U.S.A. who shared the same views as myself.

In comparing the Unitarians' relation to Christianity with that of Rissho Kosei-kai to Buddhism, I was surprised at first by the strong similarities between the two in formation, ideas, and purpose. But, thinking further, I saw that this is not surprising. If people are aware of the fact that they are directly connected with a supreme being, and pursue this connection seriously, they are all moving toward the same goal.

This feeling was strongly reinforced by the visit of Dr. Dana McLean Greeley, then President of the Unitarian Universalist Association of America, who stopped and talked with me on the way back from attending the Japanese-American Inter-Religious Consultation on Peace in Kyoto. I learned from Dr. Greeley that Unitarians have always cherished the idea of interfaith cooperation. In 1900 they organized the International Association for Religious Freedom (IARF) to assist those working toward realizing faith and freedom in various countries. In this regard their position is similar to that of Rissho Kosei-kai in cooperating with other religious organizations. Kosei-kai has directed its efforts toward the growth of the Union of the New Religious Organizations in Japan and, especially during the last two decades, has advocated interfaith cooperation both at home and abroad.

When he observed the religious activities in our Great Sacred Hall at Kosei-kai, Dr. Greeley remarked that he was impressed by this vivid demonstration of living Buddhism. Both of us sensed a strong feeling of brotherhood and even unity.

Our discussion focused on the subject of dialogue among people of religion. We agreed completely that mutual understanding is the basis of achieving harmony and peace in human society and that the basis of mutual understanding itself is dialogue.

Dr. Greeley remarked that "although men seem to live separately and individually, they have one existence in the eyes of God. We ought to always keep this in mind and do everything from the love of brotherhood. There is nothing we cannot understand mutually if we carry on our talks in this frame of mind. It should be the mission of us religionists to make efforts toward creating a human family."

I added, quoting the words of Sakyamuni Buddha:

" 'Now this triple world
All is my domain;
The living beings in it
All are my sons.'

"The whole of mankind is really one human family before God or the Buddha. Therefore we should recognize the buddha-nature that is inherent in each one of us and respect this in our dealings with each other. This, I believe, is the way to peace."

It has been a great joy for me to have many *zenchishiki,* or "Dharma-friends," such as Pope Paul VI and Dr. Greeley, not only in Japan but also overseas. These people have given me strong moral support in my advocacy of interfaith cooperation.

My encounter with Dr. Greeley bore fruit afterward. In July, 1969, I was invited to the twentieth World Congress of the IARF in Boston, where Rissho Kosei-kai was unanimously admitted to membership. An even greater fruit was the World Conference on Religion and Peace held in Kyoto in the fall of 1970.

MOVING TOWARD THE WORLD CONFERENCE ON RELIGION AND PEACE The World Conference on Religion and Peace (WCRP) grew out of many such encounters between religious leaders. Indeed, encounter itself is an important aspect of human life. Every human relation starts with an encounter. There is a saying in Japan to the effect that the meeting of strangers on the street is nothing other than the result of various *en,* from a previous life. This expresses the Buddhist view that nothing in the universe exists in isolation from other things and that all things have complicated connections with one another, carrying over from lifetime to lifetime.

I would like to add a new meaning to this view of *en* that would include in it not only conditions in previous lives but also in future lives. This makes the encounter of today doubly significant, for it is not only the result of past karma (accumulation of deeds) but also a chance to develop *en* for establishing good human relations in the future.

In the early 1960s, with the threat of nuclear confrontation hanging over the world, efforts were made to convene a "spiritual summit" with Martin Buber, Pope John XXIII, Martin Luther King, Jr., Albert Schweitzer, and President S. Radhakrishnan of India. Nothing came of these hopes; however, Dr. Greeley, together with Bishop John Wesley Lord, Bishop John J. Wright, and Rabbi Maurice N. Eisendrath of New York, persistently maintained the vision of a world conference on religion and peace. In 1965 in New York, they held a modest interreligious consultation near the U.N. Headquarters. This led to the National Inter-Religious Conference on Peace held in Washington in March, 1966, where nearly five hundred participants voted to "explore the possibilities for calling a world interreligious conference on peace in 1967, to include all the world's religious traditions."

The U.S. Interreligious Committee on Peace, which grew out of the Washington conference, sent an exploratory mission to North Africa and Asia to sound out religious leaders on the possibilities of such a world forum. As a result, the International Interreligious Symposium on Peace was held in New Delhi in January, 1968 and was attended by forty-six religious leaders from nine world religions. I was unable to attend, but on the way back from the symposium the American delegates visited Japan and on January 22 a consultation on peace was held between the Japanese and Americans in Kyoto. These delegates also recommended that a world conference on religion and peace take place in late 1969 or early 1970 and proposed that similar consultative meetings be held to work toward realizing this goal.

From this recommendation, an Interim Advisory Committee was organized, which met in Istanbul in February, 1969. The committee delegates, strongly supporting the idea of a world conference, adopted a proposal to hold the World Conference on Religion and Peace in Kyoto in 1970.

The earnest hope of many world religious leaders of involving the world religions in working for world peace was moving closer to realization. The Japan Religions League expressed its heartfelt agreement and its willingness to sponsor the conference. The world congress was now in the actual planning stage.

After the Istanbul meeting the first Preparatory Committee and Executive Committee for the conference were selected and the first Executive Committee meeting was held near Boston in July, 1969. The Reverend Shuten Oishi, the Japanese executive secretary, myself, and others represented the Japan Religions League. At this meeting such issues as the schedule of the conference, the number of participants, conference themes, and expenses were decided upon. Following the schedule set up at this meeting, both the second Executive Committee meeting and a Preparatory Committee meeting were held in December in Kyoto. Thus the principal items for realization of the World Conference on Religion and Peace had been decided by early 1970.

The attitude of people in general toward this world conference was not very hopeful. Some people criticized it, saying that no one could expect much to come of a discussion on peace by religious people. However, I think that world peace is something in which all of the four billion people of mankind must be involved. Unless nuclear weapons are totally banned, all mankind will share the same fate regardless of what particular ideological beliefs people hold.

This means that nearly four billion people are navigating a rough sea in a single ship. People must realize this and cooperate because their ship is in danger of sinking. No matter how difficult it may seem, religious people must also contribute their time and energy to this task. We might use the metaphor that however poor the land and severe the climate, unless we sow seeds, plants will never begin to grow.

What is important is to sow the seeds, even in a single square foot of land. If the seeds should die, then we will sow a second time, and this time we will make a frame or a vinyl cover for them. If we continue our patient endeavors, the seeds will surely push up shoots someday.

I believe that human beings possess the wisdom to achieve survival. Unless we believe this, how can we even go on living? Even though I may be criticized by some as a hopeless optimist, I still continue to believe in man.

THE JOY OF SOWING SEED I believe that it is the way of an active person to sow seeds positively and willingly by himself if he believes in his objectives. If he hesitates or thinks that his own efforts will be fruitless no matter how hard he may try, or if he thinks the wall of actuality will be too thick, he cannot advance toward his objective. If someone only starts *doing,* there will surely be those who follow him.

Florence Nightingale went to the battlefields of the Crimean War, as she could not stop thinking of the wounded soldiers, and took care of them without distinguishing friend and foe. This deeply moved the Swiss philanthropist Jean Henri Dunant, and caused him to found the Red Cross organization. Needless to say, the Red Cross is now greatly serving the welfare of all mankind, transcending even the boundaries of race and nation, both in peace and in war.

The reason we religionists united for this conference is the same. And what enabled it to be realized was the sowing of the seed called "contact." Through repeated contacts and talks, the time gradually became ripe. But even though we are still in the stage of just sowing seeds, it is our utmost joy that we colleagues, who are united by ideals and friendship, have been able to gather and sow these seeds.

You may understand such an idea better if you read the following remarks, which I delivered as the chairman at the opening ceremony of the first World Conference on Religion and Peace:

It is my heartfelt pleasure to have this privileged opportunity of addressing the distinguished religionists who are gathered here today from all over the world. On behalf of the Japan Religions League, the host organization to this World Conference on Religion and Peace, let me first of all express our deep gratitude to you all, whose participation has made this gathering a most significant occasion. I would also like to take this opportunity to express our thankfulness to the Reverend Kosho Ohtani, President of the Japan Buddhist Federation, for graciously accepting the call to the Honorary Presidency of the conference, thereby giving added dignity to this historical gathering.

The Preparatory Committee and the Executive Committee have been very instrumental in making the idea of this conference into a reality. We are deeply indebted to the members of these committees for their united and untiring efforts. They are Archbishop Fernandes, Dr. Greeley, Shri Diwakar, Rabbi Eisendrath, Prof. Husain, Bishop Lord, Msgr. Murray, Prof. Saiyidain, Cardinal Wright, Dr. Jack, Rev. Inada, Rev. Miyake, Rev. Nakayama, Rev. Oishi, and many officers and volunteers who have worked for this conference.

I have long cherished a hope that someday I shall meet

and discuss with those in religious fields who are working hard for peace of mind, peace among men, and the peace of the world. This dream has now been realized here and today in the form of this conference. And let me express my conviction that this gathering cannot but be a great success. Some of you may criticize me for this unqualified optimism, but allow me briefly to dwell upon my personal experiences that have led me to this conviction and optimism.

At one time, various religions, precisely because of their own convictions, were unable to cooperate and were even antagonistic to each other. But the times have changed. Improvement in means of transportation has made the earth much smaller, and progress in science and technology has made it possible for man to see his planet from outer space. In this day and age, the need for unity in the family of man is being brought home with an increased sense of urgency. It is my firm belief that religion alone can provide the motive power to create a peaceful world, not through armed might but through respect for humanity.

Indeed, the time has arrived when religions, instead of antagonizing each other because of what we once thought were religious convictions, should cooperate with each other in order to contribute to the cause of mankind and world peace, because, in the final analysis, all sectors of religion are and can be bound together by the common aspiration for human happiness and salvation. This must be our responsibility, the responsibility of us religionists who are called upon to realize on earth the will of God and the spirit of Buddha. It is for this reason that in this conference we must address ourselves sincerely to the question, "What can and should we religionists do?"

The genesis of the World Conference on Religion and Peace partially dates back to the Japanese-American Inter-Religious Consultation on Peace, held in Kyoto in January, 1968. Participating in this conference and talking intimately with religionists from abroad with whom I had no personal acquaintance, I was pleasantly surprised to discover so many of my colleagues shared the same enthusiasm, the same conviction, and the same understanding.

I have since witnessed with my own eyes and mind how this understanding has developed into mutual trust and confidence, which, in turn, have produced deep friendship, and how this has heightened into religious cooperation overcoming sectarian differences, and ultimately into making this conference a reality. This is something that cannot be achieved through self-interest or calculation. Nor would sectarianism, such as being a Buddhist or a Christian, be equal to this task. This conference has been made possible precisely because all the religionists, who are dedicated single-mindedly to the cause of human happiness, have focused all their attention on the problem of where they can cooperate and what they can achieve through such cooperation. Out of such heartwarming experiences during the two years of preparation for the conference, and out of invaluable and enthusiastic discussions with the dedicated religionists I have come to know, a deep conviction has begun to grow in my heart that this conference must be a great success in its contribution to world peace.

Some people had suggested that the conference should have met during EXPO '70, for it would attract a greater number of participants who might avail themselves of this opportunity to visit the exposition. However, let us recall the fact that the slogan of EXPO, "Progress and Harmony of Mankind," represents man's aspiration rather than a reality, and that to achieve "progress and harmony" still remains an unfinished job. And would it not be true that we religionists are called upon to lay the groundwork for this important task? We chose to hold this conference not during, but immediately after, EXPO '70 because we are guided by our religious mission of making progress a genuine and orderly

The efforts of people of religion are like incense. Although the smoke of the incense soon disappears, its refreshing fragrance lingers on to make people happier.

Rev. Niwano was received in a special audience by Pope Paul VI during the Second Vatican Council, September, 1965.

Right, Archbishop Athenagoras of the Eastern Orthodox Church greets the author in Istanbul, Turkey, in 1969.

Far right, top, WCRP II was held in Louvain, Belgium, in August, 1974. The author addressed the opening plenary session.

Far right, bottom, the inaugural plenary session of the ACRP was held at the Singapore Conference Hall in November of 1976.

◀ *Conference participants observed inter-religious prayer services at various War Memorials. The author led the prayers at the Kranji War Memorial.*

◀ *Talks with Mother Teresa, of Calcutta, were spiritually uplifting.*

The "Friendship Tower" in the Philippines was constructed in 1975 in Bataan, near the site of a fierce battle during World War II.

Young travelers on the "Youth Ship" unload a truck full of relief goods—clothes, medical supplies, and so forth—at Constitutional Hill in the Philippines in July, 1976.

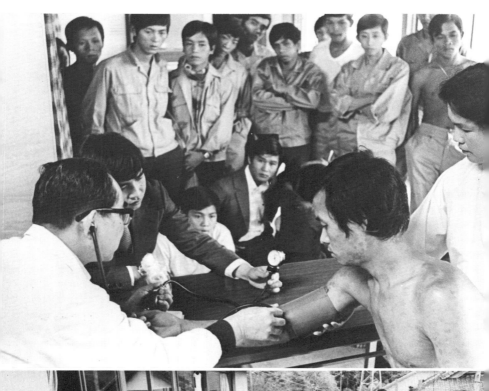

◄ *Vietnamese people receiving physical examinations at Kominato, Japan, in April, 1977.*

◄ *Vietnamese people who have been at Kominato since April, 1977, welcome newcomers in May, 1977.*

In March, 1976, Rev. Niwano was awarded the degree of Doctor of Laws, honoris causa, *by the Meadville/Lombard Theological School in Chicago in recognition of his efforts for peace and interreligious dialogue.*

In May, 1976, the author received the 1976 Uniquest *Schweitzer Award.*

The road to peace is long, but each step brings us closer to the goal.

one and of dissolving conflicts into harmony. I hope you will kindly understand how we felt in organizing the conference.

It is true that many people today are negating or neglecting religion. But, no matter whether they believe in God or not, they are, deep in their hearts, ridden by serious doubts and are asking themselves, "Is this the right way for us to live?" They are in search for a way for man to live based on a universal truth that transcends both time and space. Obviously many people, being beset with the blind recklessness of scientific and technological advances and the resultant disharmonies—pollution is one of them—that surround our daily lives, have gradually begun to reconsider their past path.

In the closing ceremony of EXPO '70 one of the overseas delegates said pointedly, "If I were forced to choose between progress and harmony, I would rather choose harmony without progress than progress without harmony." As he meant to say, the world today is full of disharmonies. While we talk complacently of the analogy of men being brothers in the same boat, we have a tragic gap between those living in abundance and those starving, nature and man, and so forth.

Of all the discords and disharmonies, those among various religions in the past should not escape our attention. We should sincerely reflect upon this fact, for, in the final analysis, it represents the lack of harmony between us and God, us and Buddha. We must first of all repent this grave sin.

Only when we start our discussion and cooperation with this repentance and reflection, can the World Conference on Religion and Peace offer real tidings for the future of mankind.

Let me close with our sincere hope that we, children of Buddha or God, will stand hand in hand and lose no time in bringing harmony into the world that is realizing world peace.

THE FIRST WORLD CONFERENCE ON RELIGION AND PEACE The first World Conference on Religion and Peace was held at the Kyoto International Conference Hall, October 16–21, 1970. Thirty-nine countries, notably including communist countries, such as the USSR, Poland, East Germany, Romania, Bulgaria, and Outer Mongolia, sent over three hundred delegates. Among the religions represented were Buddhism, Christianity, Islam, Shinto, Confucianism, Hinduism, Judaism, Sikhism, Zoroastrianism, Jainism, and Bahaism.

The gathering in Kyoto was one of the largest-scale religious conferences held in recent years, but more significant than the number of participants was the harmony in which they worked. People of different faiths, symbolized by yellow Buddhist robes, Christian crosses, white turbans, and colorful robes, all lived, ate, and worked together as they discussed their common goal for mankind.

On October 20, the fifth day of the conference, Archbishop Helder Camara of Brazil opened his speech with the following words: "Some years ago, a meeting such as this would have been unthinkable. And, let us admit, even today, each one of us is aware of the difficulties he has to face within his own congregation. The important fact is that the miracle of our being here has been accomplished by the Lord."

After the closing ceremony of the conference and the adjournment at midnight of the Executive Committee meeting, Dr. Greeley blissfully said to me, "It was a great day today, wasn't it? Excuse me! Since it is already past midnight, I should say, 'It was a great day yesterday.'"

It seems to me that the brief words of these two men expressed the meaning and fruitfulness of the conference better than a million words could have. We discussed the issues of world peace very earnestly, never losing humility toward each other as men of religion. There had been heated arguments at times as some of the delegates related such tragedies as war, hunger, and racial discrimination that were engulfing their countries. But all the participants sincerely agreed from the depth of the heart that all men and women of religion should accept one another in order to make every effort for peace.

Peace means much more than just the absence of war. Taking the position that only when the agony of poverty, hunger, and suppression of the basic freedoms of man are all wiped out from this planet will true peace visit mankind for the first time, the conference dealt with the major topics of disarmament, development, and human rights. In addition to the plenary sessions, the conference also included various meetings of commissions, committees, and subcommittees at which the participants were able to continue their discussions.

A booklet entitled *Religion for Peace* (edited by Dr. Homer Jack and published by the Gandhi Peace Foundation, New Delhi) is highly recommended for a closer, interesting in-depth look into the proceedings of the conference.

The seed had now been sown. Concrete plans to make that seed sprout were then made at the plenary session of October 21. The following resolution was adopted.

We, the members of the World Conference on Religion and Peace, resolve that:

1. The work initiated at Kyoto shall be continued in the form of a new interreligious world body called the "World Conference of Religion for Peace."

2. There should be established an international office which, in turn, should encourage the establishment of national and regional bodies consisting of dedicated men and women of various religions devoted to the cause of peace with justice.
3. Conferences, seminars, and study circles should be held at national, regional, and international levels to create a climate of opinion conducive to the peaceful resolution of all disputes between nations and within nations without recourse to violence.
4. An interreligious presence should be developed at the United Nations and at other international conferences whereby the influence of religion can be directly exerted on conflict resolution.
5. Efforts to develop the science of interreligious dialogue on peace should be continued.

We commit ourselves to these objectives and measures in the conviction that peace must no longer remain a distant dream but become a practical possibility.

It was resolved that efforts be made for a second World Conference on Religion and Peace to be held in three years. In addition, the new Executive Committee chosen during the conference decided to set up an international secretariat in New York, to be located near the United Nations Headquarters, and also to send a mission to Vietnam.

The mission to South Vietnam, the first concrete action proving the conference in Kyoto to be more than a mere festival of religious people or a publicity stunt, was promptly carried out. Five people from the Commission on International Affairs of the Japan Religions League took part in it December 18–24 of the same year. As chairman of the committee, I was the head of the group. Our goal was to get the facts about the situation in Vietnam as a preliminary stage of action allowing for Japanese religious people to unite in contributing to the peace and welfare of the Vietnamese people, based upon the spirit of the Kyoto conference.

While in Vietnam, we visited many places around Saigon and Hue, sometimes coming within only ten or twenty miles of the North Vietnamese border. We talked with various Vietnamese Buddhist, Catholic, Cao Dai, and Hoa Hao religious leaders and also visited the Foreign Ministry of South Vietnam and the Japanese embassy to exchange views and opinions. Our direct and objective observations of many places made us sensitive to the complexities of the issues in the Vietnam of that time.

The country was divided into north and south, and in addition to that antagonism, there was even hostility between the government and antigovernment forces in South Vietnam. People in the south were so divided that the confusion and confrontation even affected people of religion. Buddhists were divided into the An-Quang Pagoda and National Pagoda factions. When it was suggested that they cooperate for the sake of peace, both replied negatively, saying, "Nonsense!"

I had felt the difficulties of religious cooperation many times before, but regrettably it seemed to be exceptionally bad in Vietnam. We strongly urged that, in the same spirit of unity as we had achieved in Kyoto, the religious people of Vietnam should also learn to cooperate for the peace of their country. But the problem was a complex one.

In Vietnam, the political power that existed behind religion influenced religion itself. One leader of the An-Quang Pagoda faction, for example, indicated that it was the United States' support of the National Pagoda faction that was the main divisive force. This, I think, could have been said for the Vietnamese War as a whole. Powers other than the Vietnamese should have withdrawn their forces long before they did. It was already, by 1970, past the point where simplistic statements, such as "we are right" or "justice is on our side," had any meaning. Tragically, since nothing happened to change the situation until much later, many innocent civilians died.

We felt that it was no longer the time to discuss righteousness or ideology. It was time to step forward and solve issues from a much higher level, that of love for mankind. The earth as a part of the entire universe is but a very tiny entity, like the eye of a mosquito. This makes it ridiculous for men to fight and kill each other over such things as territory or political systems. Living on this tiny eye of a mosquito, there should be no conceivable alternative to leading our lives harmoniously on good terms with one another.

Only in religion do people take such a universal viewpoint. In order to prevent wars like the one in Vietnam, all humanity should agree with that premise of peace. This is what I felt most strongly throughout our fact-finding tour of Vietnam.

Since then, the seed we had already sown has rapidly continued to grow. In April, 1971, a meeting of officers of the World Conference on Religion and Peace was held in New Delhi. A special session on East Pakistan was held and a statement adopted. In another major step toward the realization of world peace, the WCRP also passed a resolution to send representatives of various religions to the United Nations.

At a party held after this meeting, Indian religious leaders who had attended the conference in Kyoto stood up in turn and warmly stated that the first World Conference on Religion and Peace had been "wonderful." They added: "In Japan, religions are vividly living. We are grateful for the efforts that Japanese religionists made for the conference."

It deeply impressed me that these words were not mere diplomatic eulogy but the sincere implementation of religious cooperation in the struggle for peace.

5 ON THE ROAD TO PEACE

A TOWER OF REGRET AND A TOWER OF FRIENDSHIP It has been over seven years since the first World Conference on Religion and Peace was held in October, 1970. Time flies so fast. This first World Conference on Religion and Peace was an incomparable accomplishment in the history of world religions. The meaning of the conference is truly epoch-making for those who study the history of religions.

There were various criticisms of the conference, and some people called it an "Expo of Religion" or an "Olympics of Faiths." Others, however, valued it as the "United Nations of Religions." However it was described, we were pleased with the fact that representatives of so many religions and nationalities harmoniously attended the conference, even though we do not boast of the number of participants.

International conferences and peace movements of men of religion have, in the past, tended to be confined to one specific sect or religion rather than ecumenical, and perhaps one-sided in leaning to either the American or the Russian camp. But the Kyoto conference was attended by religious leaders who, in the name of peace, transcended the barriers of national boundaries and religious sects.

Throughout history, the absoluteness that religions have claimed did not permit them to compromise. Stubborn postures were unchangeable, enabling religions to maintain the firm beliefs of their adherents. However, this also caused many conflicts between religions.

When we remember the bloody incidents of religious wars during the Middle Ages, we especially realize what Archbishop Camara referred to as a miracle—representatives of all the religions of the world gathered in one hall.

When I talk about the first World Conference on Religion and Peace in Kyoto, I should refer to the Second Vatican Council held in 1965.

2308 to 70.

What do you think this figure means?

Powerful elements of the Catholic Church have been known, throughout history, to strongly denounce any Christian denomination other than their own. Catholics had thought of themselves as the sole possessors of Truth and were proud of being the direct successors of Peter, who had been ordered to establish the church by Jesus Christ himself. At the Second Vatican Council, however, the Catholic Church, by a clear majority, adopted a declaration recognizing and respecting all other faiths. The figure mentioned above is the exact count of the vote by which the Catholic Church courageously reformed the stubborn posture it had maintained for about one thousand years.

Frankly, I want the fact to be appreciated that the church, for the first time, as a token of this ecumenical movement, invited me, a Buddhist, to the council. I would also like to say that for me, who hopes to contribute to peace by interfaith cooperation and whose so-called bible is the Lotus

Sutra, which preaches that every religion is from the same root, the encouragement of the council was an unforgettable steppingstone that gave me reason to be hopeful for the realization of a world conference on religion and peace.

THE DEATH OF IDEOLOGY   Until recently, people thought that it is ideology that forms, characterizes, and leads society. They even thought that this ideology was immutable and absolute. Therefore they easily fell into dogmatism and always aggressively adhered to antagonizing ways of thinking. However, since it has become necessary to have a planned economic system in the free world and since a system of competition and of distributing profits has even been introduced into some communist countries, ideology itself is gradually becoming homogenized. The basis of ideology is therefore crumbling bit by bit. The foolishness of struggling to cling to dogmatism has gradually been recognized by both sides.

Dr. Hajime Nakamura, professor emeritus of Tokyo University, says the following on the absurdity of killing each other for reasons of ideology: "Ideology is merely a method of conveying something ultimate. Since this ultimate is something like 'void,' it cannot be precisely expressed in words. Therefore, in order to make men understand it as much as possible, philosophy and ideology were born. Though they are imperfect, it is a fact that these philosophies and ideologies contain partial truth. If people would realize this, they would no longer kill each other defending the absoluteness of their way of thinking."

In the complex and diversified world of today, the people who realize that ideologies of the past are insufficient are those uttering, "Death to ideologies!"

We have now reached the point where it should not be necessary for one to pay attention to whether someone is right or left, capitalist or socialist. Instead of demanding that one select a particular ideology, we should struggle to search for a way in which mankind can live in harmony.

That being the case, I'm firmly convinced that the way in which religionists view the world, especially through Buddhism, will play a major role in solving the problems of our deadlocked world. When I travel overseas I often hear it said that what will save the world now is for Buddhism to join hands with and lead the scientific civilization that was born in the West. Arnold Toynbee once said, "When a historian one thousand years from now writes about the twentieth century, he will surely be more interested in the interpenetration which occurred for the first time between Christianity and Buddhism than in the conflict between the ideologies of democracy and communism." These words deeply impressed me as the words of a man who clearly sees what will really move history and be meaningful among the many things that mankind will leave for its descendants.

IN THE DEPTH OF MY HEART Now let me shift my story to more concrete matters. Recently, young people of my organization, Rissho Kosei-kai, cooperated with each other and built a "Friendship Tower" in the Philippines. Through it, they made a modest but significant contribution toward friendship between the people of the Philippines and Japan. On that occasion, the governor of the province of Bataan awarded the title of "Son of Bataan" to the head representative of the RKK Young Adults' Group. It was only a small event, and those who are not familiar with the history of the Pacific War may not be interested in it. However, for those who know that the Filipinos still harbor deep scars in their hearts because of the cruelties perpetrated by the Japanese army against Filipino citizens and prisoners of war, such as the infamous Bataan Death March, the title "Son of Bataan" should have great meaning. It was just a decade ago that people in the Philippines would sometimes spit and heap abuse on Japanese tourists.

When we remain in Japan, which is now at peace, it seems to us that the Pacific War ended more than thirty years ago. But when we visit other Asian countries and talk with the people there, we often feel as if the war has not yet ended.

With World War II as a stimulus, the abandoning of colonies by "have" nations stimulated the independence of developing countries. But the real situation of Southeast Asian countries is not yet satisfactory, since the standard of living of ordinary people is still very low. Therefore we must think more seriously about the question of what is really necessary to enable those countries to fulfill the meaning of their independence and raise their standards of living.

It was our intention, therefore, that an Asian Conference on Religion and Peace be held in the autumn of 1976. I think that we Japanese people should not be stingy and should put forth every effort to put to rest the sense of hatred toward us in the hearts of the Asian people, so that Japan will become a country that they will trust.

In July, 1975, I went to Singapore to attend the Exploratory Meeting of the Asian Conference on Religion and Peace. Some people may remember that during the Pacific War, when the Japanese army occupied Singapore, many Chinese people were arrested without being given a fair trial, and thousands of them were shot and killed. I once heard that because of this there were so many corpses floating off the shore of Singapore that the sea turned red with blood.

There is a memorial tower for the victims of that sad incident now standing in the downtown area of Singapore. At present, the attitude of the Singapore government is generous and friendly toward Japan. They say that since the pages of the past have already been turned, it is not necessary to reopen the old scars of the war.

When I visited Singapore in this friendly atmosphere, a Japanese Foreign Ministry source indicated it would not be necessary for us Japanese delegates to pay homage at the memorial tower. During the first day, however, as I was casually sightseeing in a car kindly provided for me by the interreligious organization of Singapore, I asked about a tall white tower I happened to notice behind some trees.

"That's the memorial tower for civilian victims of the Pacific War," I was told.

We stopped the car and from the depth of our hearts prayed in front of the tower.

Several days later, I had the opportunity to dine with a Singapore Chinese couple. The husband had studied at Chiba Medical University and had obtained his doctorate during his ten years of service at the Kosei Hospital. Knowing that I had paid homage at the memorial tower, the man spoke seriously to me.

"To tell you the truth, my wife's father was killed by a Japanese army machine gun even though he hadn't done anything wrong at all," the man explained. "My wife's mother was just twenty-eight years old when she became a widow with four small children, including my wife, to take care of. Since then, she's had such a difficult time that at times she wanted to commit suicide. But since she had four small children, she couldn't. She struggled desperately to raise her children. Until recently, she never even wanted to use things made in Japan. She couldn't forget the atrocities of the past. She hated Japan. But now, Reverend Niwano, it is good to hear that you have visited and prayed at the memorial tower. I have never told anyone this story before. This is the first time I'm telling the family story." I was strongly moved by his words.

It seems that the message of peace uttered by one's lips and as an ideology has already been sufficiently discussed. That night in Singapore I was keenly reminded that the purpose of our conference on peace must be to put to rest the hatred in the hearts of each man and woman and plant the seeds of friendship and a new sense of solidarity.

ORGANIZING FOR PEACE Ever since the Kyoto conference, we men of religion have initiated many movements, however inadequate. It is pleasant for us to recall that Japanese religionists, in the name of a WCRP mission, visited South Vietnam at the end of 1970. In the following year, as mentioned earlier, a WCRP Officers Meeting was held in New Delhi. On that occasion, I advocated the necessity of promoting interreligious cooperation, deepened friendship, and mutual understanding between the leaders of Hinduism, Islam, Zoroastrianism, Sikhism, Buddhism, and other religions. This helped to promote the formation of an Indian Committee of the WCRP.

Furthermore, in November of the same year, the second Executive Committee meeting of the WCRP was held in New York. At that meeting it was asserted that the second World Conference on Religion and Peace should be held in West Germany in order that the WCRP become more widely known and promoted in Europe.

In 1972, a Japanese organization called the Commission on International Affairs of the Japan Religions League changed its name to the Japanese Committee of the WCRP for the purpose of expanding and improving the conference. I was appointed the chairman of the new committee but, despite this title, have been humbly trying to be its servant instead. For instance, when there is a plan to hold an international conference, I run around trying to recruit participants or give suggestions for its preparation. But it seems that once the conference begins, the most important part of my role as chairman has already ended.

I am convinced that a role in the background as a messenger or a worker would be more suitable for me. I say this without trying to imitate the words of Jesus Christ, "Whoever would be great among you must be your servant, and whoever would be first among you must be the slave of all" (Mark 10: 43–44).

I have never thought of becoming a pillar. I think that the role of chairman of the Japanese Committee of the WCRP can never be fulfilled unless one has the determination to accept the role of being a servant to others. At the same time, I am very appreciative of the cooperation and support that I have received from the many leaders in Japanese religious circles, as well as fellow members of my own organization.

I would like to now write about the Interreligious Consultation on Japanese-American Relations that was held in Hawaii in 1972. At the consultation, representatives of both sides were able to frankly and honestly discuss the various barriers and misunderstandings that lie between the United States and Japan concerning economic issues. In this respect, it seems to have been a very meaningful consultation.

In 1971, one year before the consultation, Japanese-American economic relations were facing a serious crisis. Let me briefly outline the problem of trade between the United States and Japan. After the war, Japan resumed trade with the United States in 1949 and was importing six times as much from the United States as it was exporting. In 1969, however, this imbalance was reversed, with Japan exporting 900 million dollars more than it imported. Even though it exported appliances, television sets, automobiles, and many other things, the Japanese government put strict regulations on goods to be imported.

Perhaps some readers may remember that Japanese government policies on textile products put so much pressure on the American market that it caused about 113,000 American workers in the textile industry to lose their jobs from 1970 through 1971. Four hundred textile factories were closed down in the following two years.

These complications during the United States-Japan textile negotiations are said to have been the first signs of trouble between the two countries since the end of World War II. Had a similar situation occurred during the prewar period, it could have easily been the cause of war. In addition, during the textile negotiations with then U.S. President Nixon, the Japanese Prime Minister at the time, the late Eisaku Sato, was viciously attacked by the Japanese mass media for letting the issue of the reversion of Okinawa unfavorably affect his bargaining position in the textile negotiations. According to a public-opinion poll conducted by the *Asahi Shimbun,* one of Japan's largest newspapers, when asked about the future of Japanese-American relations, more people thought the situation would get worse before it got better. Relations were at their worst.

It seems to me that the timing of the Interreligious Consultation on Japanese-American Relations, held in recognition of such an international atmosphere, was beneficial. Among the American representatives were a couple of sharp economic experts. They sometimes accused the Japanese side of ignoring the concrete issues, causing the consultation to become somewhat exciting from time to time. All the participants, however, were religionists and wished wholeheartedly for world peace. Even though there were some heated debates during the discussions, during their free time, all the delegates were friendly and cheerful with each other. The consultation was fruitful and promoted cordial relations between the two countries.

As previously mentioned, this was at a time when the

two countries were living in a mutual atmosphere of so-called "economic war."

I included the following remarks in the speech that I gave at the opening of the consultation: "Two countries, the United States and Japan, entered into a terrible state of war thirty years ago. It is being said that there may again be a crisis between both countries, but this time from an economic point of view. I do not think, however, that the relations between the two countries are in a basic state of danger. When Japanese people hear an American say 'Remember Pearl Harbor!' they still feel sorrow and their hearts almost burst with grief. As a Japanese, I deeply repent the sudden attack on Pearl Harbor by the airplanes of the Japanese Imperial Navy. At the same time I still hope from the bottom of my heart for the confirmation and future development of friendly relations between the United States and Japan.

"I believe that we, as men of religion, must remember that the dialogue by participants at the Interreligious Consultation on Japanese-American Relations should always be based on friendship and zeal for peace, however complicated the relations between the United States and Japan may become in the future. I hope we will cooperate with each other for the sake of our future and replace the old catch phrase with a new one: 'Remember the consultation at Pearl Harbor.' "

The reason I dared to recall in my speech the expression "Remember Pearl Harbor," which has practically been taboo among the people of both countries, was in reaction to a new expression that had recently been heard in America: "Attack on Pearl Harbor by the Japanese Yen." I wanted to confront the bad image that some Americans had of "untrustworthy Japanese," so for that reason at the beginning of my speech I inserted a word of repentance for the Japanese air attack on Pearl Harbor. Then what happened?

An American friend who had stood near me during my speech later said, "Our Japanese friends should know that we Americans also repent our deep sin of having used the atomic bombs against the Japanese people." His words still remain alive in my mind.

TRANSCENDING NATIONALISM The United States is an affluent country whose citizens can easily get along without buying anything made in Japan. Nevertheless, there are still some Japanese who, because of a careless underestimation of American power and self-sufficiency, shout, "Americans get out!" These people, however, should recognize that American tolerance has limits. In the past, we Japanese thought that, because of the American liberal way of thinking and diversity of races, the United States was a country in which people could not unite and therefore could not become strong. In spite of its absurdity, some people in Japan continue to have this misconception.

America has been undergoing a wave of recession. At the Church Center for the United Nations, located just in front of the U.N. Headquarters in New York and the place where our international secretariat of the World Conference on Religion and Peace has its office, there have always been many offices of various Christian denominations. When we visited there in October, 1975, however, some of the offices were closed due to economic reasons.

Applying this to the situation of American religious organizations, it is true that the financial contributions to the WCRP from the American side are insufficient. The Japanese share is being increased to cover the American deficiency. One might naturally call this unfair, and some Japanese committee members do. But I feel it is important that one only does one's best. Even though some people think that the Japanese share, because of Japan's relative smallness compared to America, should be only equal to or less than that of America, if people insist on things like that, a lot of time and energy will be wasted and the movement for world peace, the most important thing, will not be promoted.

The first problem confronting those who wish to establish a truly peaceful world, especially men of religion, is the transcendence of nationalism. I remember what Pope Paul VI said to me when I met him: "Now is the time when the word 'neighbor' should be replaced by the word 'mankind,' and religionists should be the ones who save mankind and history."

I am a Japanese. I love Japan and am proud of being Japanese. But at the same time, I am also a religionist. Though I may be criticized for arrogance, I cannot be indifferent to world peace and the happiness of mankind. Therefore I think that it is first necessary to wrestle with the difficult problem of how to transcend nationalism. I am firmly convinced that a consciousness that transcends nationalism, and service based upon this consciousness, should be the fundamental state of mind when we discuss the budget of the WCRP. Needless to say, I too will join in the general debate.

Isn't it only natural that everyone should serve the WCRP with his or her own special ability or power? Those with great wisdom should use it to serve as religionists for world peace, as exemplars of faith for all mankind. Those who have money should be generous with it and help in that way. Those with enthusiasm should focus on constructive action, and those who are articulate should give words of encouragement to others.

America, as everyone knows, is a country of public opinion. It is no exaggeration to say that it is people of religion who are the nucleus of that public opinion. In that sense too, I am happy to have many good friends in America who are religionists and am encouraged that they are helping the cause of world peace.

In the future, there may be minor troubles or suspicions between the United States and Japan. But even if this happens, I am convinced that the ties between the religionists of the two countries, created through the WCRP, will surely play an important role on such occasions.

SEVENTY YEARS OF GRATITUDE When I go to a foreign country, since there are fewer telephone calls and visitors than when I am at home, in addition to attending conferences I have time to read books and quietly meditate during my free time. This was especially true when I went to New York in November of 1975 to attend the Officers' Meeting of the WCRP. Reflections of the past decades came to my mind while I was alone in my hotel room. Perhaps it was because my seventieth birthday, called *koki,* the celebration of which was being planned by many of the thoughtful fellow members of my organization, was drawing near.

It has been more than seventy years since I was born into this world. After ten years of searching for truth, it has been more than forty years since I encountered the Lotus Sutra and devoted myself to its practice. I can find no words to express my deep gratitude for having been able to live a life so filled with devotion. There could not possibly have been any other way of faith that could have better taught me the inadequacy of myself, the greatness of the ordinary, the joy of serving others, and the meaning of gratitude for life. Only because I have been instructed, educated, stimulated, encouraged, and supported by so many people have I been able to continue until now.

During my boyhood, my grandfather would admonish

me by saying, "Even a small insect must work for its own food. You were born as a human being so should become helpful to other people and society." When I decided to come to Tokyo, my father advised me: "Work where you have to work the hardest and longest for the least amount of money." Yoshitaro Ishihara, the owner of the store where I worked shortly after coming to Tokyo, helped me by instructing me in business. There was an old lady of Shugendo (a syncretistic belief) who helped me to understand the joy of serving others. I also am in great debt to my revered teacher, Sukenobu Arai, who was the first to lecture me about the Lotus Sutra and teach me the greatness of Buddhism. Myoko Naganuma, the late vice-president of Rissho Kosei-kai, was my best friend along the way. And my fellow Rissho Kosei-kai members always supported me in many ways. All of them are, so to speak, messengers of the Buddha, or manifestations of the Bodhisattva Regarder of the Cries of the World. They all thoughtfully and warmly helped to raise me.

In addition, there was the Reverend Shuten Oishi, who, knowing my belief that interreligious dialogue and cooperation is an inevitable necessity to the mission of Buddhists, introduced me to people of many other faiths. According to the teachings of the Lotus Sutra, all religions are of the same root or basis and of the spirit of Mahayana Buddhism. Dr. Shin'ichiro Imaoka also has been very enthusiastic in promoting mutual understanding and cooperation among world religions. These are the people who brought to me most of the motivation for the new development in my religious activities that has allowed me to humbly continue my present efforts.

There are some people who assert that there is absolutely no chance that the countries in the world will abandon their weapons. During the last ten or so years, however, many constructive agreements have been promoted, such as the Treaty Banning Nuclear Weapon Tests in the Atmosphere, Outer Space, and Underwater; the Treaty on Principles Governing the Activities of States in the Exploration and Use of Outer Space, Including the Moon and Other Celestial Bodies; the Treaty on the Non-Proliferation of Nuclear Weapons; the Treaty on the Prohibition of the Emplacement of Nuclear Weapons and Other Weapons of Mass Destruction on the Seabed and the Ocean Floor and in the Subsoil Thereof; and the Convention on the Prohibition of the Development, Production, and Stockpiling of Bacteriological (Biological) and Toxin Weapons and on Their Destruction.

We should not give up hope. There are some people who say that the realization of a peaceful world is nothing but a dream. This is a great mistake. But needless to say, there is also no reason for blind optimism. If each individual ignites the light of peace in his or her heart, to that extent a peaceful world can be realized.

Peace should not merely be preached. It is most important that movements be organized. But there are some people who think that even this is impossible. Is that really so? Many difficulties may remain, but let us look at the United Nations. Look at the European Economic Community. The people of these organizations are continuing their steady efforts for peace.

For this reason I advocate the importance of the *Sangha,* the community of believers, and, guided by that ideal, will continue to devote my small capability to the WCRP.

BEYOND DIFFERENCES   I recite a chapter of the Threefold Lotus Sutra every morning. As there are thirty-two chapters in the sutra, I finish the whole volume in a month by occasionally reciting two short chapters in one morning. This task starts my day and I never neglect it, either at home or while traveling abroad.

Once in a while room attendants enter while I am recit-' ing the sutra in a hotel room in a foreign country; I sense their reverence as they become careful as to not disturb the recitation by making noise even though they surely cannot understand the words of the sutra. I must appear strange to them as I burn incense and recite the sutra, wearing a white sash on which the Sacred Title is written in Chinese characters. However, the sacred atmosphere of prayer is conveyed and they become solemn. The differences of language and custom are transcended by their reverence.

In the WCRP, representatives of various religious groups, in turn, lead a prayer prior to every meeting. They thank the Supreme Being for the opportunity to gather, and pray that, though they themselves are of little importance, by receiving divine favor they might have a fruitful meeting. I feel that this is very meaningful as it expresses our sincere prayer that the delegates will stand on common spiritual ground even though their languages may differ.

Recently I had a talk with a Christian who had attended many international conferences. He said the following, which impressed me greatly: "In order to make a conference successful, participants should have a common basis. However, if they discuss objects of worship or their respective deity, the conference will be thrown into confusion. Therefore delegates should make a heart full of mercy the principle of mutual understanding."

I myself believe that the God in Christianity and the Eternal, Original Buddha in Buddhism are quite the same. Isn't it limiting or belittling the Supreme Being for people to add explanations that God and the Buddha, which are boundless existences, are such and such, or describe their functions and powers, or compare God and the Buddha while discussing their differences? Is it to limit the existence of the Deity that petty men frame the Deity in such a way? I believe that men can admire God and the Buddha but cannot describe or delimit them. Anyway, it is an interesting observation that the common basis of an international conference should be a heart full of mercy.

It is estimated that ten years from now the number of deaths by starvation, mainly in Asia and Africa, will reach one hundred million due to the increase in the world's population. Men of religion become terrified upon hearing this and strive to solve this tremendous problem in order to protect mankind from the population crisis. Only with a merciful mind can men of religion cooperate with each other while transcending their differences.

SPRINGING FROM DELUSION   People of different countries have different dispositions. Americans are very frank and openhearted. They speak to a person just because he or she happens to be sitting beside them in a train or bus. Compared with Americans, Germans seem to be careful. They ask questions seriously before expressing their own opinions, and they are very logical.

In 1972 I visited major religious leaders in West Germany to ask their cooperation for holding the second World Conference on Religion and Peace. When I talked with Bishop Kunst, then representative of the Protestant Churches to the government, he asked me about my view of God before I could discuss the WCRP, which was the main purpose of my visit. Therefore our discussion of religious views was longer than that of the main topic. But it was meaningful theological talk, and Dr. Maria Lücker, who was with us then, was also pleased, saying, "It was rather philosophical talk." After this religious discussion the atmosphere became very friendly and the main topic was covered smoothly. At the beginning, we felt a coolness from the Germans, but when we sufficiently understood each other, they became very friendly and cooperative. This seems to be one of the characteristics of the German people.

While traveling in foreign countries we feel the differences of national characteristics, such as the carefulness and sense of humor of the British people and the eloquence of the Indians. However, at the same time we also sense people's piousness, in other words, an attitude that can be called either the buddha-mind or the mind seeking goodness. This is exemplified by the prayers held at the beginning of conferences and through the consideration shown by hotel employees when they hear my scripture recitations. This piousness is something that binds people together, transcending almost all differences.

To put it in another way, all people worship as something holy, and revere as something great, the ultimate concern, which is invisible but exists as the original source of the universe. I feel that I well understand the reality of the saying "Every being has buddha-nature."

According to psychologists, no matter how different national characteristics may be, in the minds of children no such differences can be found. In the world of children, differences can easily be overcome and friendships quickly made. Contrary to children, aren't adults seeing things through colored glasses? Religion tries to make us see the real state of things by taking off our colored glasses and to be as innocent as children.

Zebras are eaten by lions. But in spite of this, on television we often see zebras eating grass without fear while lions are napping nearby. Why don't these zebras fear the lions? Because they know that when lions aren't hungry they never attack other animals. Unlike zebras, men are apt to jump to conclusions, as they have some ability to foresee. However, fortunately or unfortunately, as this ability is imperfect they cannot always foresee correctly. For example, if a man thinks, when he sees another person taking a nap, that the other is just pretending to sleep but is actually watching him, waiting for a chance to attack, his suspicions overcome his sensibilities and he becomes ill at ease and is tempted to try to attack the other man first.

Thus, due to man's imperfect ability to foresee—the illusion taught in Buddhism—man worries over unnecessary trifles and becomes unhappy. It is just as is said in the Lotus Sutra: "The ocean of impediment of all karmas is produced by one's false imagination."

6 A PROMISING FUTURE

APPROACHING THE SECOND WORLD CONFERENCE ON RELIGION AND PEACE   The first World Conference on Religion and Peace sprang from an idea, or to be more precise a question. We asked ourselves whether, in order to rid the world of the sense of distrust that fills people and to wrestle with the various causes that prevent peace, it wasn't necessary for representatives of the various world religions, whose mission it is to serve peace and mankind, to gather together and discuss matters concerning peace. They should become of one mind and respond to the various issues that confront religion today. Now is not the time to discuss the doctrinal differences of various religions. Because of these differences it is all the more necessary to meet, discuss, and consider our responses to the issues of our age.

Thus, through the gathering of representatives of the world religions, stimulation, encouragement, and information can be brought to those people who are striving for a peaceful world. The louder the voice crying for peace, and the more universal it is, the greater its influence will be. These were the reasons for the formation of the World Conference on Religion and Peace. However, due to lack of time, the WCRP was not well publicized in Europe and its influence was not strong.

Therefore, after the successful first World Conference in Kyoto, we wished to hold the second World Conference on Religion and Peace in Europe, hopefully in West Germany. For that purpose, as already stated, I visited Western European countries while I attended the twenty-first World Congress of the IARF (International Association for Religious Freedom) held in Heidelberg in 1972. I met with Dr. Gustav Heinemann, who was the President of West Germany; Josef Cardinal Höffner, who was the Archbishop of Cologne; Bishop Kunst; leaders of the World Council of Churches at their Central Committee meeting in Utrecht; Bernard Cardinal Alfrink, who was the International President of Pax Christi; Dr. Joseph Spae; and others, asking their cooperation for the holding of the second WCRP.

I was especially impressed that President Heinemann, who himself is a German church leader and a pacificist, made efforts for access between East and West Germany. He earnestly said that "it would be most meaningful if the second WCRP could be held in Berlin," though he added, "Because of my official position, I really should refrain from speaking like this." Therefore, pursuing the holding of the second WCRP and the cause of peace in general, I traveled extensively in Europe by automobile, train, and airplane, with the Buddha as my guide.

ENCOURAGING THE   In May, 1973, the World Conference on
UNITED NATIONS   Religion and Peace was granted Consultative Status, Category II, by the United
Nations Economic and Social Council (ECOSOC). To com-
memorate this event, I would like to express a few of my
thoughts on the U.N.

We Buddhists practice the Way, aiming to achieve spiritual peace and enlightenment, and establish the Land of
Serene Light. When we are asked what this peaceful place,
the Land of Serene Light, is, we may be able to explain by
saying that we would use a world federation, a world state,
as our blueprint. When people talk about consolidation,
Westerners say that A and B and C are different but can be
added together. On the other hand, we Japanese are said
to think that A and B and C were originally one, a whole,
and the parts can be brought back together again, rather
than be added together to form something new. The Japanese mind maintains that fundamentally, all is one.

Recently I had the pleasure to talk with Professor Masa-
hiro Mori of the Tokyo Institute of Technology, and he
made some interesting remarks. "A bacterium's actions are
always the same. If the bacterium's product is favorable we
call it zymolysis, but if the product is inconvenient we call
it decay. Man, as in this example, often separates into parts
that which was originally one, according to the level of
convenience of those parts. However, for us to give up our
differentiation and recognize that all existences and functions are one would truly be *satori* [enlightenment] as is
taught in Buddhism."

The saying "Illusion and buddhahood are the opposite
sides of the same coin" also teaches us the doctrine of Oneness, this being one of the tenets of Buddhism. This type of
thinking is easily understood by the Japanese, and raises no
antagonistic feelings in them. When we look at the world
of today, filled with confrontations based on discrimina-

tion and delusions, we feel that this attitude would be a valuable one. However, we should not forget that this style of thinking has had an undesirable effect on the Japanese in that they tend to be easily satisfied with only the theory and forget about the step-by-step methods that the world also demands.

A world state or federation would surely be the ideal organization. But in our present world we cannot overcome the egotism either of individuals or of nations, and to suddenly renounce our national sovereignty would be too difficult. However, as a step in the direction of a world state, we should realistically strive to make the existing, functioning U.N. the most powerful and rational of the globe's organizations. We people of religion must be versatile and continue our efforts to persuade individuals and nations to control their egos, to strengthen the solidarity among nations at the U.N. by searching for common interests among those nations, and to make full use of all political and diplomatic avenues available to achieve a peaceful world.

In November, 1973, I visited Kurt Waldheim, the Secretary-General of the United Nations, along with other Japanese religious leaders, and discussed the relations between the religious community and the U.N. Secretary-General Waldheim described the role of the U.N. in today's world and earnestly asked us to encourage support for the United Nations from a religious point of view. Not only the Secretary-General but also the other leading officers of the U.N. whom we met during our visit pleaded, "Even if when the United Nations speaks out on an issue it may be criticized for intervening in the domestic affairs of nations, if you men of religion energetically support the U.N., our judgments will be accepted as abiding, as they will be backed by the conscience of mankind. I sincerely ask your cooperation."

It is true that there are many criticisms to be made, but

we cannot deny that the United Nations has been very helpful in preventing another global war. It may be no exaggeration to say that this is due in no small measure to the efforts of the Economic and Social Council. This council attempts to solve problems through social means for the benefit of all mankind, while ECOSOC's partner, the Security Council, deals with problems from a political or military viewpoint. The Economic and Social Council has done a great deal of good in the past, and we of the WCRP see it as very meaningful that our organization was granted Consultative Status by ECOSOC.

PARTING THE BAMBOO CURTAIN During the first half of 1974, I was given the opportunity to visit several socialist countries, going to China in April, and in May, to Hungary and Romania.

My visit to the People's Republic of China was made possible by an invitation extended by Liao Chang Zhi, President of the China-Japan Friendship Association, and Chao Pu-chu, President of the Buddhist Association of China. I had hoped to talk with as many religious leaders as possible rather than just go sightseeing. After the cultural revolution, the position of religion in China was quite unknown, so that we did not even know how to make contact. Each time an International Officers meeting of the WCRP was held, I was asked to visit China in order to contact the religious leaders of that country, and furthermore to invite them to participate, if possible, in the second World Conference on Religion and Peace. Finally, I was invited by the Chinese to visit their country.

It was just at this time that the anti-Confucius, anti-Lin Piao campaign was occurring in China. Setting aside the anti-Lin Piao campaign, it was quite a surprise to me that such strong criticism of Confucius would appear in China, as people think of Confucianism when they think of China, and naturally of Confucius when they think of Confucianism. People in China may also have been surprised. At any rate, I was going to visit the country, so I was very interested in learning the real situation.

Before leaving Japan, people advised me not to talk about Confucius, and not to use certain words. After attending a seminar on China and hearing all this, my secretary became rather nervous. However, I thought, "Borrowed plumes are sure to come off sooner or later. It is not necessary to superficially flatter the Chinese or to become falsely diplomatic. Since they were kind enough to invite us in order to show and explain to us their country, I think it would be better to talk with them frankly and honestly in order to make our visit a fruitful one. It may not be conducive to real goodwill and friendship to flatter them and say that everything in China is wonderful."

Therefore, when I was in Hong Kong on the way to Canton and heard that thirty people who opposed the anti-Confucius, anti-Lin Piao campaign were shot in Kuangchou, I frankly and directly asked the man who took care of us in Peking whether this news was true or not. The man replied, "It could never have happened. Even during the Sino-Japanese war, we gave cooked rice to Japanese prisoners though we ourselves ate plain millet. Therefore, how can we shoot our fellow citizens just because their opinions are slightly different from ours? That must be a false rumor produced by foreign reporters."

We talked with Chinese people openly and straightforwardly. The Chinese also asked us frank questions, such as, "Do you think there is a possibility that in the next election of the Japanese House of Councillors the conservative party will be replaced by the Opposition parties?" and "Although a thirty-percent increase of workers' salaries in Japan was achieved by the spring wage-increase campaign, since the prices of consumer goods are also rising rapidly, isn't that wage increase being substantially reduced?" Sometimes I almost believed that I was back in Japan, even though I was in China and talking to the Chinese.

Concerning the anti-Confucius campaign, I said without hesitation, "Though perhaps unconsciously, haven't the teachings of Confucius been deeply rooted in and greatly affected the personality of your leader, Mao Tse-tung? As Confucianism has been handed down from generation to generation in your country, it would seem impossible to completely cast it from the hearts of the people." Confucianism has been in China for well over twenty centuries and the elderly generation seem to have been perplexed. Their reply, "We too are now studying the question," sounded honest to me. Of course my main purpose in visiting China was to meet and talk with Chinese religious leaders, who are unknown to outsiders.

Fulfilling my wishes, Chao Pu-chu was able to convene over twenty Buddhist, Christian (Catholic and Protestant), and Moslem leaders at the reception hall of the Guang Ji Si Temple in Peking, the home of the Buddhist Association of China. The meeting lasted several hours, and when it was over, Mr. Chao was also pleased, saying that it was very seldom that leaders of various religions in China gathered together, and that there were many stories that he himself had only heard for the first time. Everyone felt that the meeting had been very meaningful. The words of the Protestant representative were especially impressive to me. After saying that in the past, Western missionaries taught the Chinese to love the West rather than their own country and made them submit China to invasion by Western forces, he said, "It was regrettable that whenever one Protestant was born in China, the Chinese nation lost one citizen." Another commented, "Foreign missionaries were tools of imperialism."

I understood that the wounds in the minds of the people present were very deep, and I listened seriously to what the religious leaders said. After they had finished, I stated that since the religions of the world have now entered into a new age of mutual understanding and cooperation, it would be better to speak to the world through such channels as the WCRP, which is related to the United Nations. It would also be helpful to urge foreign religious leaders to reconsider what has been done in the past to the Chinese people. Moreover, I expressed my own repentance, as a Japanese, for the sins that the Japanese military forces had committed.

Through my discussions with these people, I came to the conclusion that it would still be very difficult for Chinese religious circles to send representatives to a universal group like the WCRP. However, I strongly feel that as a preliminary stage, communication between Chinese and Japanese religionists, especially Buddhists, should be started.

The month after returning from China, I flew to Hungary and Romania. In Budapest I talked with many Christians, including the deputy minister of the State Office for Church Affairs of Hungary, and in Cluj, Romania, I attended the Executive Committee meeting of the IARF (International Association for Religious Freedom). Unlike China, in these two countries gradual liberalization seemed to be occurring. Though the people were a little more plainly dressed than in Western European countries, the younger people were enjoying the music of popular groups like the Carpenters. They seemed to be aware of both the virtues and the shortcomings of socialism.

OVERCOMING DIFFICULTIES IN REALIZING THE SECOND WORLD CONFERENCE ON RELIGION AND PEACE

"Has the green light been turned on?"

"No, not yet."

"This is an awkward position. Can we hold the second WCRP within the next year?"

This conversation was held by some of those who were concerned with WCRP II when I visited New York in November, 1973. There were a number of problems in the holding of the second World Conference in West Germany. The Munich Olympic Games had suffered from the sudden assault by Arab guerrillas, and the country was in a turmoil. In addition, 1974, the year we planned to hold the second WCRP, was the year of a major conference of the German Protestant Church, which had already been scheduled. Many German religionists could not devote enough time to prepare for the WCRP in the very same year. These two factors were the main reasons for changing the conference site to Belgium.

There were several reasons that Belgium was chosen as the site. The country is located at the crossroads of Europe, it is the European Economic Community's headquarters, and furthermore, there is an excellent press center in Brussels, making Belgium a convenient location for those who would attend the conference.

However, for Belgian religious circles, it was not easy to accept such a big conference as the WCRP so suddenly. There were timing, economic, and physical barriers. Consequently, our plan was again faced with major difficulties, and when officers of the WCRP conversed with each other, the phrase "The green light has not been turned on yet" became quite common. We were in a difficult position. Under these circumstances, the International Preparatory Committee meeting for the second World Conference on Religion and Peace was held at the University of Louvain in Belgium in March, 1974. On this occasion, the officers of the WCRP talked with Cardinal Suenens and asked his cooperation, explaining to him the spirit and the meaning of the WCRP. It is an undeniable fact that this talk greatly promoted the chances of the holding of the conference in Belgium.

There have been many difficulties in promoting the WCRP. However, I believe the words of Sakyamuni Buddha that "the cause of all suffering is rooted in desire." I always keep in mind that man *can* transcend his egoism. When a meeting is stalled or a plan comes to be deadlocked, the faces of the delegates tend to become clouded. At such times, I try to keep my face cheerful, and say with a smile, "Nothing is impossible if the religious representatives of the world try, with good intentions, to do good. If the mind of each of us really serves the will of God and the spirit of the Buddha, we will surely receive their help and blessing." This shores up my own mind and at the same time encourages the other participants.

Today, there are many world conferences. But it seems to me that the one thing that is really important is lacking in these conferences, and this is a selfless attitude. In other words, every country takes the attitude, "I am the only exception." For example, suppose there is the proposition, "The export of weapons by major powers should be prohibited." Needless to say, all delegates will agree with this. But their real attitude, in many cases, is, "You'd better carry this out in your country, but my country will be the exception." Another example is the urging of people to save the energy resources that we are rapidly depleting. This too is agreed upon by every delegate. But when it comes time to decide who should really conserve energy, their position tends to become, "You should do it, not me." The problem of overpopulation is the same.

Unless there is a reconsideration of this attitude, however seriously discussed and important the items discussed may be, these conferences will remain nothing but conferences.

THE ABILITY TO CO-OPERATE WITH EACH OTHER After many ups and downs the second World Conference on Religion and Peace was finally held at the University of Louvain in Belgium in August, 1974.

More than three hundred religious leaders representing fifty-three countries were present. The major theme of the conference was "Religion and the Quality of Life." As this conference is quite well known by many people, I will omit here a detailed summary. But one thing I want to mention is that the European Committee of the WCRP was born shortly after this conference. The first World Conference on Religion and Peace held in Kyoto in 1970 was noted for the fact that for the first time leaders of the various religions from every corner of the world gathered in a conference. But at the second WCRP in Louvain, we stepped forward to discuss how we could work together.

Talking about the fruit of this conference, I must compliment the campaign promoted by Shōroku Shinto Yamatoyama, a fellow member organization of the Union of the New Religious Organizations in Japan. President Tazawa and his fellow leaders, who have been studying and working with us in the union, participated in the Louvain conference, as well as the Kyoto conference, and have made earnest contributions. After returning from Louvain, President Tazawa started a fund-raising campaign for the Japanese Committee of the WCRP. I would like to illustrate some examples of their campaign.

Sakae Nakanishi, a leader of the organization who also attended the Louvain conference with Mr. Tazawa, published a book on his tour to Louvain titled *Walking Among Flowers*. Mr. Nakanishi kindly donated the income on the book to the Japanese Committee of the WCRP for the fund for promoting peace. Members of the organization also donated money totaling about seventeen million yen, which they raised by quitting smoking and by restricting their diet, under the slogan "Let us save one meal and drive away one desire," in the hope that the money could be used to help suffering people in Asia.

The origin of this donating practice was motivated by a mini-conference that several prominent Japanese delegates held after their return from Louvain. During the discussion, responding to the report that one Japanese consumes the food and resources equivalent to twenty-odd people in a developing Asian country, the Reverend Sakata, President of Misogi-kyo and the Secretary-General of the Japanese Committee of the WCRP, said, "At the time of a severe famine a few centuries ago, the founder of my Shinto organization preached to his followers, saying, 'I will save others from starvation by saving a meal of my own.'" This greatly impressed the other members of the meeting. Shōroku Shinto Yamatoyama promptly started a campaign to save a meal per month in order to raise funds and to gain more feeling for the starvation of the people in afflicted areas. This campaign stimulated the youth in other groups affiliated with UNROJ (the Union of the New Religious Organizations in Japan). In Rissho Kosei-kai, too, the Young Adults' Group earnestly promoted a save-a-meal campaign.

Thus, interfaith cooperation has the power to bring forth opportunities for encounter and dialogue that nurture mutuality and development. People of religion often tend to become self-satisfied, just like the frogs in the well who are ignorant of the ocean. Those who really want to be genuine religionists will never be satisfied with the status quo, but will always keep asking themselves, "Am I good enough?" I am entirely convinced that the encounters derived from interfaith cooperation and dialogue are absolutely indispensable for people of religion.

THE PRACTICE One day as Sakyamuni Buddha was taking a
OF DONATION walk, he saw a bird eating an insect. Inspired, he was able to grasp the true meaning of the Law of Causation, which he presented to the world. Sakyamuni Buddha sought a world of harmony away from a world where the strong prey upon the weaker. We can see this harmony as expressed by the planets. They have complex orbits, but these orbits are well organized and the planets do not collide. I am convinced that man, because he too is a component of the universe, is supposed to be in harmony with that universe, and that this is entirely possible. This harmony comes only from the spirit of loving others. Where then does this spirit of loving others come from?

The fact that I exist in this world is, needless to say, thanks to my parents. The fact my parents existed is due to my ancestors.

The food that I eat, the clothes that I wear—all are made by others.

The reason I can travel throughout the world on my humble efforts for peace is only due to the strong support of my fellow members of Rissho Kosei-kai.

We can do nothing without the help and support of others. Without those others, we are not able to live. Therefore, I always reply to those who ask me "How ought man to live?" by saying, "Before I answer your question, think about why you are able to live now." Then people come to realize that they are able to live only through favors that come from outside themselves. We cannot live without those. We, as individuals, can exist only by being supported by the whole universe.

When we adequately understand this, a sense of joy and gratitude wells up within us. When this sense of gratitude springs forth, a desire to be of some help to others, to serve others, to reward others, will arise. In other words, one comes to understand that to give to others is the only real way to live!

Therefore, a donation or offering is not given in the spirit of self-sacrifice or to stir up one's fighting spirit, but is something that naturally and spontaneously springs up as a manifestation of the Law. It is the act of responding with gratitude for the favors that one has received from others. A true world of peace will appear for the first time when all people show this spirit of giving of themselves, and endeavor to be in harmony with the whole of mankind.

THE ASIAN CONFERENCE ON RELIGION AND PEACE   The Asian Conference on Religion and Peace was held in Singapore in November, 1976. It was most productive and, being an Asian-oriented conference, naturally bore certain unique features, differing in some respects from the two World Conferences on Religion and Peace held in Kyoto and Louvain. In all, about three hundred active participants from seventeen Asian and Pacific nations attended. Observers from five non-Asian countries also attended. Japan sent a large delegation of almost one hundred people.

The most urgent question in the minds of all participants throughout the conference was, "How can we act in order to further the common goal of all religions, peace?" This question underlay all the deliberations and the enthusiasm of the conference.

The present situation in Asia is highly complex, and the question of the path that we Japanese should follow will present many difficult problems. Thus the mission of Japanese religious people is very important.

I recollect what Michio Nagai, then the Minister of Education, said in his speech to the Japanese delegation before they departed for the conference: "The way of religious men is a way of suffering. I respect you men of religion as you are following the way of suffering. The way is steep. May your efforts be successful. I will sincerely pray for your success rather than congratulate you at the beginning of your trip."

There were some people who were not able to attend the conference because their governments refused them permission to leave the country. Their governments did not appreciate the efforts for peace that men of religion can make. When I learned this, I strongly felt how much remains to be overcome in bringing true peace to Asia.

The final publication of the proceedings and findings of the Singapore conference will contain the results of the conference in detail. Here, I want to discuss what we gained indirectly through the conference. The most important by-product of the WCRP was the deepening of mutual understanding and the promotion of interfaith cooperation from the religious standpoint. The ACRP promoted the same results. At home, the Japanese Committee of the WCRP had held two study seminars in preparation for the Asian Conference. It repented what Japan had done to Asian peoples during the Pacific War and tried to clarify what we Japanese men of religion could now do for peace in Asia. These seminars were of great help in deepening our understanding of several aspects of the present situation in Asia and of what role Japan should follow to be of service. At the same time, through informal discussions and spending several days together, all the participants became well acquainted. They became able to talk very frankly even about the various issues confronting them within their own denominations or organizations, as well as those thoughts on religion and peace they held in common. This naturally strengthened the feeling of solidarity among the members of the Japanese Committee.

The interfaith movement was also highly significant at the Singapore conference. The Inter-Religious Organization of Singapore has maintained good relations among its affiliated religions (Buddhism, Islam, Christianity, Hinduism, and so on) since its formation more than a quarter of a century ago. After the Inter-Religious Organization consented to be the host of the conference, its members, including young people, worked hard in preparing for the conference. Their friendliness among themselves, the harmony they showed, and their earnest devotion made a deep impression on the participants from other countries.

I was given the opportunity to deliver the inaugural address as the chairman of the Organizing Committee of the ACRP. In my address I said, "At the first preparatory meeting for this Asian Conference on Religion and Peace, a preamble for the conference was adopted. It begins with the words 'Asia is a rainbow. It has a variety of colors and juxtapositions.' In fact, Asia does have a multiplicity of colors, and many shades of diversity. There are many religious traditions and customs coexisting in the various cultures of Asia. It is true that, in some cases, these diversities complicate present situations or are the very cause of conflicts. On the contrary this diversity, just as the various instruments of an orchestra produce a wonderful harmony by expressing their respective characteristics fully, has the possibility of creating beautiful music. It depends, of course, upon our efforts."

The Inter-Religious Organization of Singapore is an example of a harmonious melody. During the conference period, the affiliated religious bodies of the IRO invited all participants to evening prayer services and dinner parties. Many elderly and young believers, both lay and monk, voluntarily served as waiters, waitresses, and cooks. They offered their warmhearted and sincere hospitality to each delegation in turn, always mindful of the characteristics of the various religions. This attitude impressed and pleased all the participants.

Interfaith prayer was one of the significant features of the conference. On one morning, the ACRP participants were divided into two groups, one going to the Kranji War Memorial for the military dead and the other to the Memorial Tower for civilian victims. Even though the participants represented different religions, they were all able to pray together, both for the war dead and for world peace. Many of the delegates had had bitter experiences during the Pacific War. Not a few had had friends, relatives, or family members wounded or killed by Japanese military forces. We Japanese prayed in a spirit of sincere repentance for what Japan did during the war. But all the participants prayed for a common desire: peace.

I was asked to lead an interfaith prayer at the Kranji War Memorial and accepted, as the Japanese delegation was large and as all its members felt a deep sense of responsibility and repentance for Japan's part in the war. We all prayed together, and I offered a bouquet of flowers. The sky was clear, and the sound of many languages united in prayer was solemn yet warm.

Participation by more women and young people than before was one of the characteristics of this conference, something that had been advocated at both the Kyoto and Louvain conferences. At the ACRP, both these groups were deeply involved and held many meetings of their own. Not only were there youth delegates, but also nearly one hundred young people from Singapore, Japan, and other countries worked on the staff and did volunteer work for the conference. These young people combined passion and energy, and their common tasks promoted mutual understanding. They worked from early in the morning until late at night, and it was not uncommon for them to have only a couple of hours of sleep. They cooperated with and helped each other, and it is because of them that the conference went so smoothly. Even during the short breaks and at lunchtime these young people talked with each other and learned from each other. They belong to a generation that has not known war, so their views and feelings are slightly different from those of older people. It is highly significant that this younger generation saw their task from a religious point of view, and pooled their efforts to work toward a common goal.

Even after the conference, friendship among the young people continued to grow. They kept in contact with each other through letters and voice-tapes. Some explored the possibility of holding a youth conference, and learned from what young people in other countries are doing. Some were even able to visit their colleagues' countries. The president of the Youth Circle of the Buddhist Union in Singapore visited my organization in Tokyo and held talks with Japanese young people on how to promote youth activities. Also, the Japanese Shinto delegation to the ACRP so inspired their fellow believers that a second group decided to go to Singapore, and I am sure they will have a very meaningful trip.

The significance of a conference to promote peace lies not in the fact that the conference is held, but rather in what that conference is able to achieve. One of the participants in the ACRP was Mother Teresa, a Roman Catholic nun whom many people consider to be a living saint for her service to the poor. Mother Teresa described herself by saying, "I attend this conference as the representative of the poorest among the poor." Her keynote speech, backed by her deeds, deeply impressed all the participants. She began her speech with a prayer: "We will say a prayer for our brothers and sisters in whose name I stand here before you: Make us worthy, Lord, to serve our fellow men throughout the world who live and die in poverty and hunger. Give them daily bread, and by your understanding love, give them peace and joy.

"I am very grateful to God to be able to be with you, and to share with you the love of our people throughout the world: the blind, the lame, the unwanted, the uncared for, the abandoned, the lepers, the sick and dying destitute, the lonely children, the unwanted children. And with them, together, to understand that we have been created for greater things—God has created you and me and them for greater things—to love and to be loved. And all the works of love are works of peace. And we need each other to be able to understand the reason of our existence: we have been created to love, and to be loved."

This is the same spirit that is found in the Conference Declaration.

I had a couple of occasions to talk with Mother Teresa personally, and found them deeply inspiring.

THE BOAT PEOPLE PROJECT The Boat People Project was a task undertaken as a direct result of the Asian Conference on Religion and Peace.

During the ACRP, information on some Vietnamese refugees was brought to the attention of the delegates. A small boat with about twenty Vietnamese aboard, including women and children, had been floating at sea. As it had been badly damaged, the boat was sinking and the people were faced with the danger of death. Fortunately a passing tanker had rescued the refugees, but they had not been allowed to disembark at any nearby port and were still on board the ship, which was lying at anchor off the coast of Singapore. Upon hearing this news, a group of delegates volunteered to meet and talk to the refugees.

The news was conveyed by word of mouth. Many participants expressed deep concern for the fate of Indochinese refugees drifting aboard small boats in the South China Sea, for their SOS signals were ignored by many ships simply because no government was likely to give them asylum.

Many people were moved by the refugees' sad situation, and the conviction that the conference should not overlook this problem became widespread. This belief was expressed by the conference participants in various parts of the Conference Declaration, and in commission reports on human rights it was one of the most crucial topics of the conference.

The following resolution on the refugee issue was proposed and adopted at the final plenary session:

Resolution on Indo-China Refugee Relief

The Asian Conference on Religion and Peace shall explore all possibilities to help the refugees from Indo-China, who have been constrained to live on small islands in the South China Sea, utterly destitute of daily necessities and provisions for life, and also those who are floating on the sea in small boats with little food and fuel, facing hunger and death at any moment.

We are concerned for their peace and dignity, as well as for world peace. They are part of us.

Immediate actions have to be taken for those who are crying for our help.

Thus, the conference, in consultation and collaboration with the WCRP International Board, which will meet immediately following this conference, will work out the necessary steps to help solve these problems by mobilizing the spiritual and material resources available to us.

At the meeting of the International Board of the WCRP, which followed the Asian Conference on Religion and Peace, it was decided that a relief committee should be set up within the WCRP. The Japanese Committee of the WCRP decided to contribute $60,000 to initiate a fund for the rescue of the refugees, with other donations to be raised by religious organizations throughout the world.

We Japanese religionists felt that, being men of religion, we should do what we could even though there would be many difficulties in carrying out our task. This project would be our mission alloted by God and the Buddha. The proposition that the Japanese Committee would offer the initial funds was readily accepted and seems even to have moved delegates from other countries. Representatives of America, Canada, Australia, and other countries also pledged to make the utmost efforts for the success of this project, both in fund-raising and in urging their respective governments to let them receive more refugees in their lands.

A group of people immediately sprang into action. Meetings were held with the representative of the U.N. High Commissioner for Refugees in Kuala Lumpur, the French Ambassador to Singapore, and representative of the U.S. Embassy in Singapore, and the conclusions were reported to the WCRP International Board. In brief, it was decided to try to rescue refugees floating in small boats, reportedly numbering several hundred, for the monsoon season was approaching. The refugees would be disembarked at safe locations either temporarily or permanently and, when temporarily, would be helped to find countries where they would be given permanent asylum. It was emphasized that this was an urgent and humanitarian task, not a political one. The resolution of the WCRP International Board also stated that "the U.N. High Commissioner for Refugees will be consulted at every step."

Thus the Boat People Rescue Project was begun. The WCRP International Board appointed a relief committee headed by Professor Yoshiaki Iisaka of the Japanese Committee of the WCRP and including a representative of the Singapore Inter-Religious Organization. The relief committee was authorized to charter a ship and immediately began to rescue the refugees. Concurrently, attempts were and still are being made to have the five ASEAN countries, plus Japan, the U.S.A., and Australia, provide shelter for those rescued while their requests for resettlement are being processed.

Concerning the Indochina Refugee Relief Fund, the WCRP's International Board adopted a resolution requesting that "various national and international nongovernmental organizations allocate emergency relief funds for the rescue of Indo-Chinese refugees now drifting in small boats on the China Sea." As a result, more than $200,000 was donated by religious groups around the world, much more than was anticipated at the outset. We were deeply moved that conscientious people throughout the world so quickly and generously opened their hearts in the cause of humanity. In January the rescue project swung into high gear. Two ships, the *Roland* and the *Leap Dal,* were chartered, and a large number of refugees was picked up; the total number rescued was about 550.

During the course of the project there were some unfortunate moments caused by inadequate communications or by misunderstandings, both between the people involved with the rescue effort and between the rescue workers and the mass media. There were also a few people who were not faithful to the spirit and the principles of the ACRP and WCRP. The situation finally stabilized and returned to the direction in which the project had initially been aimed after sincere efforts by all the workers and the kind cooperation of the U.N. High Commissioner for Refugees.

All the refugees on the *Roland* and the *Leap Dal* were eventually able to land, and they have been gradually transferred to various countries for permanent settlement. WCRP and ACRP declared the Boat People Project ended. Along with this project, I would like to mention modest efforts made in Japan.

From spring through early summer of 1977 there were many Vietnamese refugees aboard small boats on the open seas. Some newspapers reported that the number of refugees amounted to about five thousand. Very few passing ships and tankers picked them up. However, some ships could not overlook these miserable people and brought them to Japanese ports. The Japanese Committee of the WCRP, in collaboration with the UNHCR in Japan, made efforts, as part of the Boat People Rescue Project, to find temporary asylum for the refugees, appealing to various religious bodies in Japan. We in Rissho Kosei-kai received more than fifty people at Kominato in Chiba Prefecture and another forty at Takahama in Fukui Prefecture, housing them in our facilities.

Through these people the terrible situation of the refugees was made known in concrete fashion. Many of the refugees had fled their mother country at night on small fishing boats of five or ten tons. Coming to the open seas, such as the South China Sea, they had asked help of passing freighters and tankers. So as not to be ignored, the boat people would row out in front of a tanker or purposely destroy their engines in trying to gain a freighter's attention. The forty people who came to Takahama, belonging to our Wakasa Branch, told us that they had left Vietnam at three in the morning in mid-June on a boat 14 meters long. On the second day, their boat's engine broke down. They began their nineteen-day ordeal afloat with only fifty coconuts and a small amount of rice. The daily ration per person was a spoonful of rice and some coconut rind. While drifting, three died. An eleven-year-old boy and a nine-year-old girl died of starvation. Another boy dived into the sea when he became delirious. The others, fortunately, were rescued by the Greek freighter *Krios,* but even a half day later, their fate would have been in doubt. Their boat had sunk until it was only 20 centimeters above the surface of the sea.

There were many difficulties in taking care of these people. First there was the language barrier. None of us was able to speak Vietnamese, and none of them spoke Japanese. Finding an interpreter was not easy. Whenever someone fell ill, it was a great problem to find out just what was wrong. Differences of climate, way of living, culture, and customs also sometimes blocked smooth service. However, we were very happy to see smiles on the refugees' faces after their ordeal at sea.

The volunteers among our fellow believers in Rissho Kosei-kai who took care of the refugees gathered precious experiences. They were able to communicate with the refugees heart to heart. Warmheartedness and sincerity are always the best language. The refugees seem to have relaxed in their new home. Caritas Japan, a Catholic body, has more experience in this field, and as they started to take care of these refugees at their facilities we learned from their experience. With the increase of refugees coming to Japan, Tenrikyo, an organization of Shinto origin, also received some dozen refugees at their facilities. The staff and members of the churches where refugees are staying have experienced at first hand what the WCRP movement really is.

It may be too soon to draw any conclusions about the refugee project, as it is not yet complete. I would rather say that consideration and efforts by people of religion with regard to the refugee problem have only just begun and should be continued in various ways. However, I can at least point out what we have learned through tackling the project, and list some achievements.

1. There is significance in the very fact that the WCRP took concrete action as an urgent humanitarian task. Though some discord and setbacks were experienced, this project opened a new direction for peace conferences of men of religion, which had tended to lead only to further conferences.

2. Through this project, the WCRP has been able to deepen the impact of the refugee issue on world opinion, to lend impetus to the efforts of various governments, and even to vitalize the action of the U.N. on this issue.

3. It was confirmed that world religious bodies would willingly cooperate and donate funds without hesitation for a meaningful project that really serves mankind.

4. In the world today, relief action cannot be carried out effectively unless religionists and secular experts cooperate closely. With regard to this project, there was tremendous cooperation, assistance, and even guidance from various sources, such as service organizations, including the Malaysian Red Crescent Society, the offices of the UNHCR, diplomatic agencies of various countries, mass media, and information media. In Japan, too, taking this project as an occasion, liaison and coordinating machinery to promote cooperative activity was formed by several agencies, such as the Associate Officer of the UNHCR, the Japanese Red Cross Society, Caritas Japan, Tenrikyo, Rissho Kosei-kai, and the Japanese Committee of the WCRP. Such cooperative efforts should be increasingly expanded and effectively organized for the future.

5. This project has been made possible by interfaith cooperation. At the ACRP, those who first proposed taking up the issue were Protestants and Buddhists, and the delegate who moved that the conference set up an offering box

in front of the conference hall and call for offerings was a Shintoist. When the project officially began, people of almost all religions participated in some way. This is a promising sign for future activities as people of religion.

PAVING THE WAY FOR THE THIRD WORLD CONFERENCE ON RELIGION AND PEACE When the Boat People Rescue Project reached its final stage, the International Officers meeting of the WCRP was held on July 11 and 12 at the Church Center for the U.N. in New York. There, serious discussion on how to prepare for WCRP III was initiated. It was decided that WCRP III be held in 1979 after thorough preparation in order to make the conference differ from the two previous conferences by holding regional conferences and by mobilizing ample support at the grass-roots level. Representatives of bodies representing the three major faiths of the United States attended: the president of the U.S. Catholic Conference, the president of the National Council of Churches of Christ in the U.S., and the executive secretary of the Synagogue Council of America. The words of these prominent figures encouraged all who were present at the meeting. Thus, the WCRP movement has now become a cooperative one interreligiously, internationally, and intercontinentally. "One can do nothing alone—but until one makes a start, nothing at all can be done." But now there are many "ones" who have started to do something. This, I feel, is a promising sign for future activities for the peace and welfare of mankind, even though our individual capacities remain limited.

CHRONOLOGY OF
MAJOR ACTIVITIES

1954 *March 5:* appointed a member of the Religious Juridical
Persons Council of the Ministry of Education. As chairman of
the Union of the New Religious Organizations in Japan, participated in a nationally viewed television program on the religious situation in Japan.

1958 *July:* traveled to Brazil to participate in the fiftieth anni-
versary celebration of the arrival of the first Japanese immi-
grants to that country. Then made a trip to observe the religious situation in North and South America. *July 19:* awarded
the Medal of Honor with Dark Navy Blue Ribbon by the
Imperial Household of Japan for his contributions to society.

1959 *October 10:* published *Hoke Kyō no Atarashii Kaishaku*
(Buddhism for Today: A Modern Interpretation of the Threefold Lotus Sutra) in Japanese.

1961 *November:* published *Ningen Rashiku Ikiru* (The Richer
Life) in Japanese.

1962 *May:* again appointed a member of the Religious Juridical Persons Council of the Ministry of Education.

1963 *July:* published *Mugen e no Tabi* (Travel to Infinity) in
Japanese. *September 14–October 24:* visited several European
countries as a member of the Peace Delegation of Religious

Leaders for Banning Nuclear Weapons. Met with many government and religious leaders and had an audience with Pope Paul VI, to whom he presented a peace proposal.

1964 With wife and eldest son, traveled to Buddhist holy places in India.

1965 *January 5:* appointed executive director of the Japan Religions Center. *September:* invited by the Vatican to attend the Second Vatican Council in Rome as a special guest. *November:* made chairman of the Union of the New Religious Organizations in Japan.

1966 *July:* published *Ningen e no Fukki* (Return to Humanity) in Japanese. Participated in the Asian Peace and Anti-Nuclear Arms Conference in Tokyo.

1967 *July 28-29:* participated in the second Asian Peace and Anti-Nuclear Arms Conference in Tokyo. *November:* published *Ningen o Sodateru Kokoro* (Home Training for Spiritual Betterment) in Japanese.

1968 *January 22:* attended the Japanese-American Inter-Religious Consultation on Peace in Kyoto. *May:* published *Travel to Infinity* in English. *September:* completed publication of the ten volumes of *Shinshaku Hokke Sambu Kyō* (A New Interpretation of the Threefold Lotus Sutra) in Japanese.

1969 *February 10:* published *Bukkyō no Inochi Hoke Kyō* (The Lotus Sutra, Life and Soul of Buddhism) in Japanese. Attended the meeting in Istanbul of the Interim Advisory Committee for the first World Conference on Religion and Peace (WCRP), and was elected to the Preparatory Committee. Had an interview with Patriarch Athenagoras, the spiritual leader of the Eastern Orthodox Church. *April 3:* appointed chairman of the Japan Religions League. *May 12:* visited Rev. Hotta, high priest of the Shingon Buddhist sect, on Mount Koya. *July:* made chairman of the Commission on International Affairs of the Japan Religions League. *July:* participated in the first Executive Committee meeting of the WCRP in Boston. In the same city attended the twentieth World Congress of the International Association for Religious Freedom. Elected a trustee of the association. Then traveled to Europe, visiting Canterbury, Secretary-General Eugene C. Blake of the World Council of Churches at the WCC headquarters in Geneva, and the Vatican, where he invited the Pope to attend the WCRP. *August:* lectured at the

National Conference of the World Federation of Religionists for World Peace at Mount Minobu, site of the grand head temple of the Nichiren Buddhist sect. Conferred with Rev. Fujii of the Nichiren Buddhist sect. *November 15:* published *Ningen no Ikigai* (A Worthwhile Life for Man) in Japanese. *December:* attended the first Preparatory Committee meeting of the WCRP in Kyoto.

1970 *April:* visited the headquarters of Tenrikyō, a Shinto organization; the Kiyomizudera temple, head temple of the Kita Hossō Buddhist sect; and the Nishihonganji temple of the Jodō Shin Buddhist sect. *October 16–21:* served as cochairman of the first World Conference on Religion and Peace, held in Kyoto. After the conference, a Prayer Assembly for World Peace was held at the Fumon Hall of Rissho Kosei-kai in Tokyo. *December:* visited South Vietnam in the interest of peace in Indochina. Made a fact-finding tour and donated relief goods to the people of Vietnam.

1971 *January 1:* a prayer service for world peace was held in the Great Sacred Hall of Rissho Kosei-kai in Tokyo. *April:* traveled to India to attend the WCRP officers' meeting. *October–November:* attended the Executive Committee meeting of the WCRP in New York. *November:* published *The Lotus Sutra, Life and Soul of Buddhism* in English. Erected memorials to the war dead on Saipan and Guam.

1972 *April 4:* appointed first chairman of the Japanese Committee of the World Conference on Religion and Peace. *May:* published *Heiwa e no Michi* (A Buddhist Approach to Peace) in Japanese. *June 13–27:* participated in the Inter-Religious Consultation on Japanese-American Relations in Hawaii. *August 12–30:* traveled to West Germany to attend the twenty-first World Congress of the International Association for Religious Freedom. Met with President Gustav Heinemann of West Germany and religious leaders to exchange views on holding the second World Conference on Religion and Peace. *November:* published *Hito Mina Kokoro Ari* (A Collection of Nikkyō Niwano's Conversations) in Japanese.

1973 *March 14:* attended the first National Inter-Religious Consultation for Peace in Kyoto, sponsored by the Japanese Committee of the WCRP. *March 29:* Dr. Michael Ramsey, Archbishop of Canterbury, and *March 30:* Joseph Cardinal Höffner, Archbishop of Cologne, visited the Rissho Kosei-kai headquarters in Tokyo and conferred with Nikkyō Niwano. *April:* reelected chairman of the Union of the New Religious Organizations in Japan. *November 13:* cited by the National Police Force for work toward crime reduction. Visited the United Nations headquarters in New York as head of the Interreligious Peace Mission sent by the Japanese Committee of the WCRP. There, talked with UN Secretary-General Kurt Waldheim and other high UN officers. Also held discussions with American religious leaders.

1974 *February 1:* prayed at the Ise Shrine for the success of the second World Conference on Religion and Peace. *February 10:* Rissho Kosei-kai sent relief goods to refugees in Laos and Cambodia. *March 13–14:* attended the second National Inter-Religious Consultation for Peace in Tokyo. *March 15:* publication of the Threefold Lotus Sutra in modern Japanese. Appointed cochairman at a Preparatory Committee meeting, held in Belgium, of the second World Conference on Religion and Peace. Received an award from the Tōfū-kai, an organization devoted to helping lepers. *April:* took office for the second time as chairman of the Japan Religions League. Visited the People's Republic of China at the invitation of the China-Japan Friendship Association and the Buddhist Association of China. *May 4:* chosen vice-chairman of the twenty-eighth General Assembly of the United World Federalists of Japan. Traveled to Hungary and Romania to attend the Executive Committee meeting of the International Association for Religious Freedom and to deepen friendships with the leaders of the association's member groups. *August:* attended, as cochairman, the second World Conference on Religion and Peace, held in Louvain, in the suburbs of Brussels. *September:* visited Pope Paul VI in the Vatican and, as head of the Japanese delegation, reported on the WCRP.

1975 *March 5:* was awarded the degree of Doctor of Laws, *honoris causa,* by the Meadville/Lombard Theological School, a graduate school affiliated with the University of Chicago. *March 13–14:* attended the third National Inter-Religious Consultation for Peace in Kyoto. *April:* Rissho Kosei-kai sent a peace delegation of young members to the Philippines and presented a "Friendship Tower" to that country. *April 26:* the Japanese Committee of the WCRP established a

Peace Lyceum. *July:* participated in a Preparatory Committee meeting of the Asian Conference on Religion and Peace in Singapore. *August:* attended the twenty-second World Congress of the International Association for Religious Freedom in Montreal. *October:* published *Shoshin Isshō* (Lifetime Beginner), *Fukuju no Umi* (The Ocean of Blessings), and *Hokke Sambu Kyō Nyūmon* (A Primer of the Threefold Lotus Sutra) in Japanese. Attended the International Officers meeting of the WCRP in New York. *November:* Rissho Kosei-kai began restoration of the That Luang temple in Laos, at the request of the Laotian government. *December:* Rissho Kosei-kai sent a peace delegation of young members to Rome at the invitation of the Vatican.

1976 *February 23:* attended the World Fellowship of Buddhists conference in Bangkok. *February 27:* attended a Preparatory Committee meeting of the Asian Conference on Religion and Peace in Singapore. *March 9–10:* attended the fourth National Inter-Religious Consultation for Peace in Tokyo. *March:* published *Buddhism for Today: A Modern Interpretation of the Threefold Lotus Sutra* in English. *May:* presented with the *Uniquest* Schweitzer Award for 1976 by the editorial board of *Uniquest* magazine in the U.S.A. for his proven dedication to the cause of world friendship and peace. *June 12–13:* served as president of the eighth Congress of the Japan Religionists for the World Federation in Tokyo. *June 15:* visited Rev. Kurozumi at the headquarters of Kurozumi-kyō, and Rev. Miyake at the Konkō-kyō headquarters. *July 6–7:* attended the first advance study meeting of the Asian Conference on Religion and Peace. *July 24:* lectured at Enryakuji temple on Mount Hiei. *August:* published *Niwano Nikkyō Jiden* (The Life Story of Nikkyō Niwano) in Japanese. *September:* attended the second advance study meeting of the Asian Conference on Religion and Peace in Tokyo. *November 25–30:* acted as president of the first Asian Conference on Religion and Peace in Singapore.

1977 *March 15–16:* attended the fifth National Inter-Religious Consultation for Peace in Kyoto. *April:* completed restoration of the That Luang temple in Laos. At the request of the United Nations Rissho Kosei-kai accepted thirty-four Vietnamese refugees who had been drifting at sea in a boat.

May: Rissho Kosei-kai accepted eighteen more Vietnamese refugees. *July:* Rissho Kosei-kai accepted an additional forty Vietnamese refugees. *July 9–16:* attended the International Officers meeting of the WCRP in New York.